SPLITTING UP
without falling to pieces

SPLITTING UP
without falling to pieces

Jan Kaa Kristensen

JKK Books

SPLITTING UP without falling to pieces

Jan Kaa Kristensen

© 2021 Jan Kaa Kristensen & JKK Books

This book is a translation of the book "BLIV SKILT uden at gå i stykker" published by Dansk Psykologisk Forlag, Copenhagen, Denmark.

Translated by Mark Kline.

Layout: GrafiskGenvej.dk

Front-page: Undine Vilde

First edition, 2021

Paperback ISBN: 978-87-972896-1-7

E-book ISBN: 978-87-972896-0-0

CONTENTS

About Not Falling to Pieces

This book is for the many divorced parents struggling to create an adequate working relationship (see box page 14) for the benefit of their children.

Even though divorce has become a normal event in life (almost half of all marriages don't last), to many people it doesn't feel normal, or easy, either. It's a demanding, destructive upheaval in their lives. Naturally, this also applies to unmarried couples who split up. Studies have shown that 46% of all divorces end in conflict, and 12-15% of them in major conflicts (Children's Rights National Association, 2016; Sander 2012).

A large majority of children make it through a divorce just fine. According to researchers, 80% of all children do well after a divorce, compared to 90% of children in a traditional nuclear family (Ottesen, 2010). Research also shows that what's most important for children during a divorce is how well parents cooperate with each other (see Amato, 2010; Bilenberg, 2013). That is why I hope this book can inspire those of you about to be divorced to make good choices for your children, yourself, and your future ex, so all of you get through the divorce as smoothly as possible.

To write this book, I talked to many people in various stages of the divorce process who were involved in several types of divorces. They gave me invaluable feedback, to the extent that what was important to them became central to the book's themes and stories. It could not have been written without their input, and I am grateful to them for trusting and opening up to me.

This book is not a recipe for a good divorce, and for good reason; divorces differ significantly from each other, and what works well in one, doesn't in another. But I hope it can lead you to a better place and to a clearer understanding of yourself, your ex, and your children, so you can steer all your lives in a positive direction by the choices you make.

One important point made in every chapter: it's imperative to take care of yourself, so you'll have the strength and energy necessary to be a parent to your children and get along well enough with your co-parent. For many people this isn't easy, by any means; they forget about their own welfare. This book is a friendly reminder to remember.

The book is structured to give you an overview of the various areas affected by divorce. You can read the chapters most relevant to your situation and skip other sections you don't believe apply to you.

There are questions at the end of each chapter that you may want to ask yourself. They can help you discover what's important to you in the chapter. You'll also find a special section at the end of each chapter, "Pitfalls," where subjects or themes dealing with what's most likely to harm a collaboration are taken up. After mirroring yourself in the stories, you might choose to avoid these traps.

A great deal has been written and discussed about divorce. Two narratives are very common: one treats divorce as something liberating and natural, while the other considers it to be wrong and harmful to children. The purpose of this book is to shift the focus away from divorce itself to how to make a post-divorce collaboration work as smoothly as possible, to the advantage of everyone involved. It's important for a couple to be able to cooperate. The same applies after a divorce. How can you work together if your ex has hurt you deeply, though? There is no simple answer to this question. But this book attempts to show you how to get through a divorce as well as possible, without anyone falling apart.

The various stories central to this book are all fictional, none of the people mentioned are real. The accounts have been inspired, however, by many of the people and families I've met professionally.

It's also important here to say a few words about the final chapter in the book, "When Other Circumstances Are at Stake," which deals with situations where special circumstances make collaborations particularly challenging. It might be a child with special needs. It might be a long, drawn-out conflict that appears impossible to resolve. Or it might be that one of the parents is particularly vulnerable, which affects his or her ability to be an adequate parent. It's important to keep an eye on situations that present unique challenges.

What is a "satisfactory" collaboration?

A satisfactory collaboration is one in which children are doing well and parents are able to cooperate with each other as if they were co-workers, even though they may not like each other. People may not like some of their co-workers, either, but they can work with them.

If the breakup has been difficult, it's important for parents to put aside the troubling emotions involved that can get in the way of cooperating with each other. It's a hardship for children if the atmosphere is strained to the extent that their parents can't exchange important information about them. The children then have to hold their lives together all by themselves, which overwhelms them and leads to problems.

When people get divorced, they can no longer interfere with each other's way of parenting. Children can handle parents doing things differently, as long as the parents are okay with it. If each parent can accept the other's dissimilar views on upbringing and caregiving, children will adapt and make their lives work in the realities of two distinct families. It can in fact be a strength, because children then learn to navigate various family cultures and discover the strengths and weaknesses in them.

A satisfactory collaboration is also built on good, clear agreements. See Chapter 10, page 129.

CHAPTER 1

Accept Your Emotions and Take Responsibility for Your Actions

CENTRAL IDEAS IN THIS CHAPTER

- Divorce is an exhausting upheaval in a life.

- Intense emotions challenge your ability to think clearly.

- Maybe you are overwhelmed by emotions – or you avoid them.

- Take responsibility for your own emotions and actions.

This chapter deals with how you can handle the difficult emotions involved in a divorce. It's important for the well-being of your children and yourself that you find a way to stay calm when under pressure. **This is also important when you have to work together with your children's co-parent. Even though divorce has become widespread and common, it feels anything but normal to the adults and children going through it. Divorce is a demanding upheaval in people's lives, and it involves a lot of time and energy. For most people, divorce unleashes many distressing emotions that have to be dealt with. Sidsel and Benjamin's story is a good example.**

Sidsel and Benjamin

Sidsel and Benjamin had a baby, and from day one it was extremely rough on them; their little boy had colic and cried all day long. They grew more and more exhausted, and unfortunately their network wasn't broad or tightly-knit; they had no one close by who could step in and relieve them. Sidsel yelled at Benjamin because she didn't think he was doing his fair share. He felt she was way out of line and unfair to him, that she was overlooking how much he was doing to keep the family afloat. Sidsel and Benjamin's breakup was difficult.

Benjamin had had a clandestine affair with a co-worker. Sidsel found out about it when she happened to notice the emails between them. She then threw Benjamin out of their rental apartment, of which she was the primary tenant. To begin with, he wasn't allowed to see their son, because he had betrayed her and the baby. Sidsel was enraged, hurt, and very unhappy. Benjamin was embarrassed; he felt guilty, but he was also a bit relieved about no longer having to keep his secret.

Divorce is a Major Upheaval in Our Lives

For most of us, a divorce seriously disrupts our lives, and for many it becomes a crisis. The processes that people go through with death and divorce are similar in many ways, but they also differ in one important aspect. When someone close to us dies, that person is no longer physically present. With divorce, our former partner is still around, and we have to cooperate with him or her when our children our involved. We become emotional during shared activities, on exchange days when the children leave to stay with the other parent, and when joint decisions concerning the children have to be made. Many people experience the time just after a divorce as especially challenging, and when our former partner finds someone new, emotions can erupt again.

Especially in the first few years after the divorce, Sidsel missed her son terribly when he was staying with Benjamin. She was deeply affected by the very chilly atmosphere between her and Benjamin on exchange days. It's natural and understandable that divorcing someone we were close to and with whom we have children is an enormously emotional experience. At times, our emotions run away with us.

Intense Emotions Make it Difficult to Think Clearly

When we're in the grip of emotion, our ability to think clearly and make rational decisions can suffer. A divorce is particularly challenging in its first phase, because we're in a state of crisis. And when that happens, we can believe that our emotions and reality are the same thing. For example, when we are angry at our ex and hurt because of the divorce. This is of course particularly likely if an affair is involved.

Sidsel was hurt and angry about Benjamin cheating on her and lying to her so many times. She threw him out, and he was not allowed to see the baby. She was overwhelmed by tormenting emotions, and she told

*her friends that Benjamin was a psychopath who was damaging both
her and her child. She felt she had no choice but to keep their child away
from him. Sidsel's anger and distress left her unable to distinguish between Benjamin as her ex and his role as the father of their child.*

If we only listen to our emotions, we tend to generalize. A person
is either good or bad; there are no gray areas, no nuances. That's
how Sidsel felt: Benjamin is a bad husband, and therefore he's a
bad father for our child, so I have to protect my boy from him as
much as possible. This is how intense emotions stand in the way
of making sensible choices. They can blind us to the needs of our
children. Sidsel and Benjamin's son was still happy spending time
with his father, and he needed a strong, healthy relationship with
him. Sidsel pulled herself together, and after a short time she realized that her son needed to see his father.

The Emotional Window of Tolerance

Whether it comes from within ourselves or from others, emotional pressure makes controlling our emotions difficult. When we are
in a state of harmony and feel strong and energetic, however, emotional pressure is much easier to deal with. To understand how
this works, try examining your emotional window of tolerance.
When you are inside the window's frame, you are calm and can
separate your thoughts from your feelings. You can listen to what
your co-parent is saying and decide whether or not you agree. You
can have a constructive conversation.

When you experience heavy emotional pressure over a long period of time, you rise above the window. That is, your nervous system is activated, and you feel physical discomfort and irritation,
perhaps. Suddenly you can't distinguish your thoughts from your

emotions, and the latter end up controlling you. You hardly hear what the other person is saying; instead of listening, you're thinking of how to respond. You might even shut down and break off the conversation and walk away, because you feel so bad.

It's particularly challenging when you find yourself in situations you have no control over. A divorce you didn't choose can be very tough to take. Your physical and emotional foundation is also under pressure, because the divorce has consequences for your relationship with your ex, your children, your network, your house or apartment, and your financial situation.

Therefore, it's natural that you react emotionally. Your nervous system is in alarm mode, because the foundation of your life is changing. You probably feel unsettled and anxious, that everything around you seems chaotic. You might become overwhelmed by rage, hurt, sorrow and loss. You might also feel a sense of relief and guilt. No matter what, you'll have your own unique way of reacting.

FACTS ABOUT THE EMOTIONAL WINDOW OF TOLERANCE

Emotional activation

You are above your emotional window of tolerance

- Your nervous system is in alarm mode.
- You're unable to listen to what the co-parent of your child is saying.
- You feel overwhelmed by emotions, and you scold and criticize, or
- You feel overwhelmed by emotions and protect yourself by fleeing.

You are inside your emotional window of tolerance

- Your nervous system is calm.
- You can listen to what your co-parent says without becoming defensive.
- You can think clearly without your emotions controlling you.

You are below your emotional window of tolerance

- Your nervous system breaks down.
- If you have been above your emotional window of tolerance for a long period of time, your nervous system
- becomes overloaded and shuts down for a while.
- You lack energy and feel exhausted and depressed.

(Adapted from Nordanger, Øystein, and Braarud, 2014)

The emotional window of tolerance differs from person to person. It's deeply embedded both in your genes and in the caregiving climate you experienced when you were a child. Try thinking about what your own window of tolerance looks like. When are you calm and in a state of harmony? When do you lose control of yourself? What triggers this loss of control?

Do you fight or flee?

When you are under emotional pressure for a long time, you react by using one of the basic human survival strategies: you either fight or flee.

When you choose to fight, you're protecting yourself emotionally. As a child you might have found that if you fought long enough, you were seen and understood. You might yearn for the other person to do just that, to see and understand you.

Choosing to flee is another way to protect yourself. You might have learned that you can best shield yourself from distressing emotions by trying to avoid them, by running away from them. But the energy you use in escaping from your emotions drains you, and your nervous system is activated anyway.

This extra pressure on your emotions strains your ability to keep calm and restricts your tolerance window. Your fuse is shorter, while the risk of exploding with rage or running far away increases.

Sidsel chose to react by attacking and fighting. She pushed Benjamin out the door after he'd packed a suitcase. Benjamin backed off, and several days went by before he contacted her again. He missed his son, and his son missed him. The fact was that he'd often avoided conflicts over the years. Usually, he'd turned silent and pulled away whenever Sidsel got angry.

These reactions are completely normal. According to attachment theory, how a person reacts is formed in childhood, during which survival strategies for handling emotional pressure are developed. The risk of someone not taking care of their emotions is that their tolerance window becomes smaller.

If you have been stressed out for quite a while, you run the risk of collapsing emotionally if you don't take care of yourself. Being trapped in your emotions demands a great deal of energy from your nervous system. When you find you can't flee or fight your way out of the situation you're in, you may feel helpless and incapable of making a decision. You don't have the energy to go on, and you might even become depressed if you don't receive enough support from your network or get professional help. This is why it's important to find various ways of taking care of yourself (see Chapter 3). It's also important to emphasize that nearly everyone recovers quickly when they receive support; their crisis lasts only a short while.

Sidsel broke down emotionally after a few months of intense anger and pain. Benjamin and Sidsel went into couples therapy, to decide if they could get back together, or if they should try for a good working relationship after their divorce. They chose the latter. After the decision was made, Sidsel fell apart again for a while. She felt helpless, empty. But with the help and support of her network, she soon got back on her feet.

Two Paths For Working Through a Crisis

Divorce can be seen as a grief and crisis situation. The newest research in this area describes two paths for working through a crisis (Schut and Stroebe, 2010). One leads into the past, one into the future; the former is about dealing with loss, the latter focuses on building a new life. It's important that the process switches between the two paths, because this makes it easier to get through a crisis.

Why is it that some parents can handle the crisis and end up just fine, while others can't? There are various explanations for this, depending on the individual. How you were treated as a child when you were unhappy is definitely a part of it, but only a part. Generally, it can be said that the better the role models you've had for handling a crisis, the easier it is for you to ask for help when you need it.

Your ability to deal with stress and crises is only one factor. Among others are: how did the breakup happen? What are the challenges in connection with the divorce? How are the children reacting? Are there other things causing you stress? What are your options for seeking support in your network?

It was particularly difficult for Sidsel to deal with Benjamin's infidelity, but fortunately she had some good girlfriends who helped support her emotionally when she crashed. It was a different story for Benjamin. He soon got on with his life and moved in with his new girlfriend. She got pregnant, and his life primarily revolved around his new family. He had very little to do with Sidsel, and he seldom talked about her with their son.

FACTS ABOUT ATTACHMENT

Our attachment to our parents is important for how we handle stress as adults.

As parents, we draw on our early experiences with our own parents, how well they took care of us both physically and emotionally. The level of basic trust we experience in our early relationship with our parents forms the basis of our own ability to handle stress and crises. If our parents were good at emotionally mirroring us, we feel more self-assured and can handle emotional pressure more maturely. We become less emotionally reactive.

About a third of all parents, however, have a less secure foundation, which makes them more vulnerable to the emotional pressure common to the birth of the baby, especially if the baby isn't doing well.

It is entirely possible that by gaining experience in life, and perhaps by seeking therapy, we can get better at calming ourselves when under pressure.

Take Responsibility for Your Own Emotions and Actions

An important part of the work of getting through a divorce is taking responsibility for your behavior toward your ex. First, it's important to consider how you react when you're under pressure. Do you tend to run away when the going gets rough, or are you more likely to fight? No matter what, it can be good to get away from what you usually do, to try something different. It's completely okay to need some distance from your ex for a while, to have time to do some necessary thinking and to take care of yourself, as long as you cooperate to create consistency and compatibility in your children's lives in two homes. Here are three suggestions to help you with this process:

First, be aware of your physical reactions when you're about to lose your temper. Do you feel it in your stomach, in your head? Do you clench your fists? What causes this reaction? Do you walk off, or do you get mad and go for the attack?

Secondly, recognize the situations where your emotions are most intense, so you'll know when you're about to get worked up. In this way you can learn what situations or what things your ex does that push your buttons.

Finally, be aware of the things you do that make your ex explode. Can you act or speak in a different way, so you don't fall into a negative pattern of interaction with them?

When you have to work together with your co-parent, it's important to give them – and yourself – space, while you're both checking out how you feel and how to react to the emotional pressure you're under. Here it's also totally okay to pull back for a while. You need to take care of yourself and give yourself time to deal with your reactions. Likewise, it's important to give your co-parent the same consideration. In this way you can each take responsibility for your part in the negative pattern.

In many ways we are role models for our children when it comes to how to handle a crisis in our lives. Children can handle a difficult and demanding period, as long as things turn out okay.

For a while Sidsel needed to see a therapist, to help her calm herself down when things got difficult between her and Benjamin. Meanwhile, he was having a hard time cooperating with Sidsel. While on sick leave because of stress, he became aware of how much of a burden working with her was, so he also began seeing a therapist. The sessions helped him to talk about the difficult thoughts and emotions he'd been carry-ing around inside.

PITFALLS

If You Think The Other Person Is The Only One At Fault

When a conflict becomes deadlocked, it's almost always because one or both parents believe it's all the other's fault. They think that if the other parent would just change the way they are doing something, the problem would be solved. Seldom is it that simple, however.

If you think your co-parent is the only one at fault, you rob your-self of the opportunity to improve your collaboration and thus make everything better for you, your ex, and your children; you won't be able to find out why your co-parent reacts the way they do, and what lies behind it; and you also won't realize how you manage to light the fuse that sets off their behavior.

In the vast majority of cases, both parents are involved in creat-ing problems and, therefore, both parents bear a responsibility to help solve them.

QUESTIONS TO ASK YOURSELF

- How do you react when you are under emotional pressure? Do you flee, or do you fight?

- What is it your ex does that sets off your most extreme emotional reactions?

- What do you do that sets off the most extreme emotional reactions in your ex?

- What strategies do you have to calm yourself down when you're under emotional pressure?

CHAPTER 2

Find a Realistic Level of Cooperation

CENTRAL IDEAS IN THIS CHAPTER

- At the beginning of a divorce, you often find your-selves in very different places in the process of breaking up.

- You need time and energy to be ready to cooperate.

- Find a realistic level of cooperation.

- Special challenges can arise when your ex finds a new partner.

- What does a satisfactory collaboration actually mean?

This chapter is about how to handle emotionally the initial stages of divorce and establish a satisfactory collaboration with your ex. Divorce can be described as a "goodbye-and-hello process," where you say goodbye to your relationship as partners and hello to co-parenting and cooperating with each other on issues concerning the children. This process requires that you work on yourself, which takes time. It's a very stressful period. Breaking up unleashes intense emotions in you, your ex, and your children, while at the same time a crucial decision might have to be made about who will have primary custody and what the visitation rights will be. Should you and your ex choose joint physical custody, or should the children live primarily with one parent? On top of all this, your daily life and routines will change, and it can all be very difficult and exhausting.

Rosa and Allan

Rosa and Allan had been together for ten years, and they had two children, eight-year-old Mattias and six-year-old Julie. For a long time, Rosa had been unhappy about Allan working too much and never being "present" when they did things with the children. Rosa had criticized Allan a lot, but eventually she gave up and gradually grew distant from him. In her mind, she said goodbye to him. And on the day she decided to tell him she wanted a divorce, she felt a great sense of relief. She was finished with fighting for the marriage.

It was an enormous shock for Allan. At first he was angry and hurt. He felt that in the last few months in particular he'd really pulled himself together. He had noticed, however, that she didn't yell at him as much anymore and that she had suddenly begun saying no to doing things together. She preferred being with her girlfriends to going out with him to see a movie, for example.

Allan reacted intensely to her wanting a divorce, and the children became very upset, which made Rosa feel guilty. But she was also angry at Allan for being so distracted and distant in their married life and toward the kids. She had already planned where she was going to move, and she'd gotten advice on what a good visitation rights agreement might entail. Allan was in a crisis. He felt powerless and so enraged that he could hardly contain himself. He couldn't afford to live in their house alone, so they were going to have to sell it. He was afraid he would have little contact with the kids if she got her way – she wanted them ten days out of every two weeks.

To leave and to be left

As in Rosa and Allan's case, most divorces are asynchronous: one person leaves and one person is left. It's not a mutual decision.

There's a big difference between being the leaver and the leavee. The former has often been dissatisfied with the relationship over a long period of time and has tried many times to change it. Dissatisfaction creates frustration, as it did for Rosa, and thoughts about divorce become more common. A grieving process begins before a divorce actually happens. You begin dismantling your feelings for your partner and become cooler and more distant. When you tell your partner you want a divorce, at first it's a relief. You become less on edge, and you don't have to fight any longer to keep the relationship going or dread the conversation about wanting a divorce. Another emotion that may show itself is guilt, about making the kids unhappy and how friends and family might not sympathize with your decision. Other emotions that may pop up are anger and sorrow that the decision had to be made. All in all, often it's a jumble of emotions: relief, guilt, anger, sorrow.

Rosa went through an entire litany of emotions. She was very relieved, but at the same time she felt guilty that Allan was so shocked and miserable about it. She also felt terrible that the kids were unhappy. Shortly after, she went through periods of doubt, wondering whether she'd made the right decision, and occasionally she even missed Allan when she thought about the good times they'd had together.

The person being left feels quite differently. It often comes as a shock when they are told their partner wants a divorce, and at first they are filled with contradictory and mixed feelings. The couple may experience dissimilar emotions, and they may differ in how much room the emotions take up in their lives.

Allan hadn't begun letting go of the marriage. He still cared for Rosa. He hadn't suspected that she wanted a divorce, and the fact that she'd already decided enraged him, made him feel helpless. His nervous system went on red alert. It wasn't his decision, and there was nothing he could do to change it. The decision also had enormous consequences for how he would be living his life from then on. Where he would live, how much time he would have together with his children. He couldn't understand why Rosa had chosen to ruin the family, and he was deeply hurt that she no longer cared for him as he did for her.

Rosa was calmer after she told him her decision. Allan needed time and help from his network to settle his nerves.

It's important to know that these emotions and reactions are totally natural and understandable, because your relationship is changing: instead of a couple, you're now becoming co-parents. You also need to know that this process will probably take a long time – maybe a year, or even longer – before your new lives feel genuine.

Time and Distance Give You Room to Work Together

In an asynchronous breakup such as the one Allan and Rosa went through, many people need distance at the start. They need time to adapt and get used to their new situation in life, especially the ones who have been left. They need time and room for their nerves to simmer down, so their emotions don't set the agenda for working together with their ex.

Too much contact can lead to situations where anger and hurt dominate communication. It can set off an escalating conflict, which makes it more difficult to establish a new relationship focused on cooperation for the sake of the children.

Time spent alone can be used to work on your emotional reactions to the divorce; unprocessed anger and hurt may lead to demonizing your co-parent and getting deadlocked in a broken collaboration. See also Chapter 8, "Seek Help When It Becomes Difficult to Cooperate."

A Job to be Done Alone

How long it takes to get to where you can work with your ex varies from person to person. It depends on how hard you've been hit emotionally by the divorce, and how good you are at calming your nervous system when under emotional pressure, as we've seen in Chapter 1.

If the breakup has been very tough on you, it can be particularly difficult to take responsibility for the painful sense of betrayal and powerlessness you feel. You might need quite a while to recover, and for some it's also necessary to seek professional help and support.

It took much effort for Allan to calm down enough to be able to be in the same room as Rosa without his emotions running away with him. Finally, his boss helped set up several sessions with a psychologist, which helped him get through the initial stages of the divorce and cooperate better with Rosa.

Many newly divorced men and women go through a period where it's torturous to be in the same room as their ex for any extended period of time. Difficult emotions pop up. The breakup is still so new that time and space are needed to get used to the new situation in their lives. Both practical and emotional help and support from others may also be needed to gather the strength necessary to adapt to their new lives.

It's important you don't completely break off contact with your ex. You need to talk about the children and all the practical things, dividing everything up, etc. Your children need their parents to be able to work together okay; therefore you need to find the right balance in your contact with each other. You also need to realize there will be a change in how much you need to work together as you both adapt to the breakup.

Find a Realistic Level of Collaboration

When you go from being a couple to ex-partners and co-parents, the challenge is finding a realistic level of collaboration. It's also a question of how close a relationship you should have with your ex.

When a couple breaks up, sometimes one or both of them dream of converting their marriage or partnership into a friendship. Often the motivation is to help the children as much as possible, by doing lots of things together.

Rosa had in fact dreamt about her and Allan being friends, and she couldn't understand why Allan was so angry and was putting so much distance between them. At first he wanted as little as possible to do with Rosa, and he gave her the cold shoulder on exchange days. In time Allan began to relax, and once in a while they could all have dinner together.

Rosa, however, wanted the four of them to be able to take vacations and celebrate Christmas together and share a meal once a week. In other words, she had lofty ambitions for their collaboration.

This level of collaboration is too high for many people. Very few co-parents can make this work, and often they're couples where both partners agreed to break up. It's important to remember that the level of collaboration can change, and it's also important to give yourself and your ex space for a while, as long as you can still work together to help your children mature and be happy and healthy.

If you both agreed to get a divorce, the situation is easier to begin with. You might make plans to do a lot of things together, and maybe you've promised each other to keep living in the same neighborhood. Both of you might want to remain friends, and that's nice for your children, but it can also be difficult for them to understand why you're not still a couple, if you really are good friends.

PITFALLS

When One of You Finds Someone New

You may be able to work together just fine for a long time, and as co-parents you might get along great when you do things together with the kids. But that can change quickly when one of you finds someone new.

When Allan found a new girlfriend and wanted to introduce her to the children right off, it led to a crisis in their co-parenting relationship. Rosa became emotional. Allan didn't want to celebrate Christmas together, and he said no thank you when she invited him to eat with them. Allan also wanted to move in with his girlfriend, which meant that he and Rosa wouldn't be living so near to each other as they had before. This was a problem with regards to their custody agreement, because Rosa felt the kids would be too far away from their school and friends when staying with him. They couldn't resolve this issue, and they had to go to the district to put together a new visitation rights agreement.

People may have the best of intentions in wanting to change a couple relationship into a friendship, but it can be more than tricky to pull it off. A person who finds someone new often wants to put more distance between them and their ex, and to accomplish this, a close friendship has to go through changes. It can be hard for an ex who hasn't found someone else. Things that didn't use to be a problem suddenly become a source of conflict, such as when one of the co-parents wants a change in the number of dinners together, the shared vacations, or the agreement to live in the same neighborhood. The one left alone might have a greater need to talk about the children and what's going on in their daily life, whereas the other now has someone else to talk these things over with; therefore their need isn't the same as it was before.

Many people experience this change in their relationship as the "second divorce," because the breakup now feels more real, the relationship more distant.

Children don't need their mother and father to be friends. They can get along fine with the type of parental collaboration that can be described as collegial, where they show respect to each other. Research has shown that the atmosphere of the collaboration is vital to children's well-being. Children sense the mood between their parents, and if the parents have a good, collegial manner of working together, with a relaxed atmosphere, that's more than good enough. Parents should therefore be aware of how to help create the best possible atmosphere when together. It's possible that one of them would like to be closer, but if the best solution is a more distanced and collegial relationship, one that puts less stress on the other co-parent, that is what's also best for the children.

Of course, it's completely okay to be good friends after a divorce. As a goal, though, it's too ambitious for many people.

When Allan found someone else and moved in with her, this "second divorce" unleashed a crisis for him and Rosa. They went through a long, difficult period, during which Rosa struggled because her ambition of remaining friends with Allan had failed. They had no choice but to forge a more distant relationship, and this made her feel angry and powerless.

QUESTIONS TO ASK YOURSELF

- Are you the one who left, or did your partner leave you?
- How have you taken care of yourself emotionally after the breakup?
- What level of ambition do you have for being able to work together?
- What is good about your collaboration?
- What do you wish could be better about your collaboration, and how can you make that happen?

CHAPTER 3

Take Care of Yourself

CENTRAL IDEAS IN THIS CHAPTER

- Take care of yourself, so you can support your children.

- Find your own way to calm your nerves.

- Use your network.

- Seek professional help when you feel you're stuck in a rut.

- Be a good role model for your children.

This chapter focuses on why it's important to take responsibility for your own well-being, and how to do it. It's vital that you take this seriously, because taking care of ourselves enlarges our window of emotional tolerance and helps us do a better job as parents. At the same time, it gives us the strength and energy to avoid pushing our co-parent's buttons, thus allowing us to sidestep the destructive patterns of interaction we often get caught in. When we're under emotional pressure, we can be quicker to criticize our co-parent, who then returns the favor or slams the door and leaves. Which leaves both of us feeling more frustrated and with less energy for ourselves and our children.

Rosa and Allan (cont.)

As mentioned in the last chapter, when Alan found a new girlfriend, Rosa was emotionally overwhelmed. She felt helpless and angry. And she was very surprised at the strength of her emotions, because she was the one who had decided to get the divorce. The transition from being friends after the divorce to a more distant, collegial relationship was difficult for her. Allan's intense reaction to Rosa wanting a divorce eventually led him to get help from a psychologist, but this wasn't the only way he took responsibility for himself; he also started a physical training program to help get rid of his anger.

Help Yourself Before You Support Your Children

When you get on an airplane, you're always told to put on your own mask before helping your children with theirs. The principle is the same in the time immediately after a divorce, as well as in many other situations.

To prevent an exhausting battle in a divorce, you first have to focus on yourself. You need to find a way to calm your nerves, to free up the necessary strength and energy to be there for your children and avoid becoming too angry with your ex.

At first it was difficult for Rosa to take responsibility for her emotional reactions after the "second divorce," when Allan had found someone else. She felt justified in being angry at Allan, and she thought he was letting the kids down when he moved farther away and didn't want to get together with them for dinner as often as before.

In connection with the divorce, Allan also had a very difficult time taking care of himself. Things started going badly for him at work, he began arguing with his co-workers, and finally his boss had a talk with him. He encouraged Allan to seek professional help, to help him "put his own oxygen mask on." Which he did.

Taking Care of Yourself Expands Your Window of Tolerance

Taking good care of yourself is important, because it expands your window of emotional tolerance. When you take a serious look at yourself and your nervous system's reactions, you become more aware of how to stay calm and in balance during particularly stressful situations.

If you keep an eye on yourself that way as part of your daily routine, you'll always be alert to what might stress you out, which helps you prepare for such situations. You'll probably find it's easier to deal with them, and you might be able to handle being around your ex more, without stepping outside your tolerance window. You'll also be quicker to sense when that's about to happen.

Find Your Own Way of Calming Yourself Down

For many people, divorce is their first major life crisis. They didn't realize they could feel so angry, hurt, and helpless. In a crisis like this, you'll draw on the strategies you developed as a child when you experienced intense emotions. These strategies might be useful and appropriate, but they might also be unsuitable and leave you vulnerable. It's a strength if as a child you learned to seek help and support from your parents or other caregivers, because this means that you'll automatically seek help when needed as an adult. On the other hand, if you learned to deal with painful emotional situations by yourself, maybe by avoiding your emotions, dealing with a serious life crisis as an adult can be particularly difficult.

No matter which strategies you use, it's important to consider how to find peace and harmony within yourself, to find a space where you accept your new situation. There are many ways to do this; there's no one right answer for everyone.

After a while, Rosa realized she was going to have to accept the situation. Her nervous system had become so overloaded that she had trouble sleeping, so she went to group therapy for the divorced. Along with five others, she investigated her reactions to divorce and mirrored herself in the others' reactions. She discovered she wasn't the only one who felt helpless. She was also inspired to do good things for herself. One that worked well for her was to listen to a particular song that expressed some of the emotions she by then was more than familiar with.

Allan found inspiration at his therapy sessions, and he also began running, which helped him stay in shape and gave him the opportunity to think about the conversations in therapy. After a run, he felt calmer and more relaxed. It was especially helpful on exchange days when he took the kids back to Rosa, days when he sometimes fell into a black mood. He missed his kids terribly.

Support and Help From Your Network

The help and support of a network is important to many people. It can be enormously challenging to suddenly be completely alone with the job of parenting, without being able to take a break and catch your breath. You may need someone who can take over temporarily when things get tough, to give you time for yourself or perhaps take care of practical matters. It doesn't have to be a long time; even an hour can help you pull yourself together.

In general women are better at asking for help and support from family and people they know, and at verbally expressing difficult emotions. Men are more at risk of an emotional collapse after a divorce. For this reason, the Danish Centers for Men have developed specialized programs for men who are having problems after a divorce. Read more about the importance of networks in Chapter 7.

It was difficult for Allan to find emotional support. His bowling team didn't talk about things like that. In a way that was nice, because while they were bowling, he wasn't thinking about the divorce or Rosa or the kids. But it felt good when a close friend who had gotten divorced a few years earlier asked how he was doing.

When Professional Help is Needed

Some circumstances in a divorce put extra strain on those involved. Infidelity, for example, can deeply hurt and enrage a partner and destroy a sense of trust. Other examples are money problems, a house that can't be sold, and a network that shuns one of the partners.

For some people, these challenges end up with one or both partners needing extra help and support for a while. A psychologist or psychotherapist can be of help to some. Others may find therapy groups for the divorced suit them better, while still others might need more practical help and support to get on with their lives.

Good Role Models for Our Children

We parents are role models for our children. Showing that we can handle our life crises, that we can work together in a civil manner, creates a solid foundation for them. They become strong and robust enough to handle the challenges they will face in their lives, including when they too become parents. Children can handle a life crisis, but only if we as parents show them how.

The work of taking care of yourself can't in itself solve the problems in a collaboration, but it helps you be as good a parent as possible.

Good Advice for Taking Care of Yourself

- Draw on your network for emotional support and an occasional respite.

- Seek out situations that provide a timeout from the divorce.

- Seek professional help when needed.

- Avoid or shorten situations that create more stress.

- Stay physically active.

- Make sure you get a good night's sleep.

- Do things that you find relaxing and help you re-charge your batteries.

- Form a plan for taking good care of yourself.

One of the first things we forget when under intense emotional pressure is ourselves. We forget to take good care of ourselves when we most need it, which can send us into a negative spiral of increasing stress and dwindling energy for our children and life in general. This is why it's important to plan how and when to focus on your own well-being. Usually this requires some sched-uling and shuffling around, especially if you have small children.

Rosa was inspired by others in her therapy group to draw up a plan to take care of herself. She started playing volleyball again, something she'd loved doing before she had kids. She went to see a play with an old girlfriend, and later on she began dating, too. During this time she felt more and more on top of things, and her collaboration with Allan began moving in a better direction.

PITFALLS

When Your Ex Doesn't Take Care of Herself/Himself

A question I often hear in my conversations with divorced parents is, what should they do if their co-parent isn't taking responsibility for their emotional reactions to the divorce? In most cases it's not a shunning of responsibility; more often it's that they can't figure things out, especially when the difficulties in working together have been going on over a longer period of time. The person hasn't learned how to settle their nervous system down. It may also be that the co-parent has been hit harder by the divorce, that they feel they've been deserted, and therefore they need a long time to heal.

Regardless, it's painful to watch. The co-parent is moving in the wrong direction, to where they are less able to be a decent parent and hold up their end of a satisfactory collaboration.

It's not easy for the parent who is good to herself/himself. This parent needs to take extra good care, given the situation, to ensure they stay within their window of tolerance. They need to be able to act and think rationally and be aware of the children's needs. Many have to lean on their network as well as seek professional help and support.

Often it's a difficult and demanding process to accept that your co-parent can't take care of herself/himself, which means they aren't always able to care for the children you had together. You might not be able to change the situation, either. Naturally, you might get angry and frustrated with the co-parent and be unable to see anything positive in them. Here it's important to remind yourself that once you were in love with this person, that they do have good qualities, but they've been hit in a very vulnerable spot and lack the ability or courage to seek help.

At this time it's vital to be the best parent you can be and support the children, because they can sense your co-parent isn't doing well. They need someone to take over, so they don't have to bear the extra burden themselves.

Your children also love the parent who is struggling, and it's important when talking about that parent to help the children understand his or her behavior, without condoning it.

What you were never given as a child can be an enormous challenge to pass on to your own children, if you don't possess the necessary emotional strength.

Staying loyal to your co-parent while also acknowledging to your children that the co-parent's behavior isn't appropriate can be a major challenge.

QUESTIONS TO ASK YOURSELF

- What good things will I do for myself in the next six months?

- Who can I turn to for emotional support?

- What can I do physically to be less stressed?

- Where can I go for a break from my divorce?

- Who can help me with practical matters when I need a timeout?

TO MEN IN PARTICULAR:
SEEK HELP AND SUPPORT TO GET THROUGH A DIVORCE

Many men find it difficult to ask for help and support during a divorce. And many of them don't receive the emotional support they need (Kristensen, 2014).

This is why some of them develop a serious personal crisis.

Some countries offer free help to men; in Denmark, it's available from Crisis Centers for Men, which have set up therapy groups for those going through a divorce.

CHAPTER 4

Create Your New Life

CENTRAL IDEAS IN THIS CHAPTER

- Give yourself time to get comfortable in your new situation.

- Get used to a new daily rhythm.

- Acquire new abilities as a parent.

- Welcome new relationships.

This chapter deals with how you as a divorced parent should also work on building a new life and a new identity. Many people are surprised by how stressful this can be, how it can unleash many contradictory emotions.

With regards to the two paths for working through a crisis from Chapter 1, the perspective that looks forward is just as important as the one that looks back. It gives you the opportunity to put painful emotions on pause for a while, to focus on developing new roles, a new identity, and new relationships.

Katja and Kasper

Katja and Kasper broke up after fourteen years as a couple. They had two children, six-year-old Josefine and four-year-old Carl. They both felt they had grown apart, plus they also had very different political beliefs. Katja was a day care center teacher, voted left-wing, and was very involved in political work aiming to increase the number of teachers in day care centers. Kasper was an accountant and voted right wing. He believed money was best left in people's pockets. They had been fascinated by their differences when young, but now the same traits were a source of argument and alienation.

They agreed to break up, and they chose a 7/7 custody agreement, in which the children lived for a week at a time with each parent. Tuesday was their exchange day. They sold their house, and Kasper bought a smaller one, while Katja moved into a rental on a residential street close to Kasper's place. Even though they saw eye-to-eye on the break-up, the decision wasn't easy.

New Framework

When you have to make a new life, you're also creating a new framework for it. By focusing on the framework, you look to your future. Your relationship with your ex completely changes in a physical sense; they won't be present on a daily basis in your new situation. The process of building a new framework is a natural and necessary part of handling the crisis, and is every bit as important as emotionally accepting the breakup.

Katja felt the framework of her life had changed significantly. Not only were the physical aspects different; they were also much worse in quality. Splitting up with Kasper forced her to spend quite a bit of money at IKEA on furnishings. And she missed some of the things Kasper got when they divided their belongings.

Katja got a shock in the first month of her new life, when she exceeded the limits of her overdraft account. She was used to having a lot more money to spend, and she realized she was going to have to manage her finances better. She'd had some expensive habits, had bought the best quality in supermarkets and specialty shops, but now she would have to shop more in discount stores. The habits were hard to break, but she had no choice.

Kasper earned quite a bit more than Katja. He had a good grip on his financial situation, and he took out some good loans and was soon settled into his new house. He was the practical type, and he quickly adapted to his new situation.

The biggest challenge for him was cooking. At first he bought convenience food, and during the weeks he had the children, they ate pizza too often. One day Josefine said she was tired of pizza; she wanted the food she and her brother ate at home with their mother.

New Rhythm – Freedom and Responsibility

A newly divorced parent's daily life changes radically. There's a totally new rhythm: weeks with and weeks without children. In the former, you have a new identity as a single parent. You may experience positive emotions of freedom, of not having to compromise. Of being able to decide everything. At the same time, you face the new challenge of being an exhausted parent without the help and support of your partner; you can't talk to them about emotions and situations and the more practical aspects of parenting. All this is a natural part of creating a new identity.

It's normal to miss your children yet feel a sense of relief on the days without them. You have free days to take care of yourself and recharge your batteries, so you're able to give them your time and attention when they return.

Settling into a new rhythm in her life was a major challenge for Katja. Her week with the children was filled with responsibilities. There was quite a bit of extra pressure, and she thought it was hard, especially right before dinner, without Kasper's help. Once in a while she lost her temper and yelled at the kids. The day before their exchange day, she was often exhausted, and she felt guilty about looking forward to sending the kids over to their father. But she seriously needed the days by herself.

After they were gone, she slept late and enjoyed her freedom, but soon she began to miss the kids and felt restless. She didn't know what to do with her time. Gradually she began to go out with her girlfriends, yet she felt an emptiness. It helped when she began planning out her free weeks. She began to enjoy her time alone.

Kasper faced the same challenges in finding a new rhythm. He was very active and present when the kids were there, but when they were gone, he found that he didn't like how suddenly quiet it was. He became restless, the hours seemed to creep by. The first few months in particular were very tough on him. It helped when he started riding his mountain bike in the local bike club, and he contacted some old friends he could hang out with, so the time without the kids would go by faster.

Developing New Parenting Abilities

When you have to stand on your own two feet and shape your new identity, you also need to develop new abilities as a parent. This is part of the forward-looking path that helps you get through the divorce. Most likely you will swing back and forth between missing the capabilities and help your former partner provided, and feeling relieved that now you're the parent you wanted to be, without having to compromise or discuss everything.

It was difficult for Kasper to be alone with the kids. It was particularly tough when Carl and Josefine argued, because usually Katja had dealt with that situation. He'd called Katja a few times for some advice, even though it was a bit embarrassing to him. He'd wanted to show her he had everything under control. He also needed to be a better cook, so they didn't have to eat pizza all the time. Gradually he learned, and Carl and Josefine were happier with what he fed them.

A major obstacle for Katja was handling her personal finances by herself. Kasper had always taken care of that. She had to set aside time to make out a budget, now that she had to be much more careful with money. She couldn't afford as many vacations as before, for example. Also, all the upkeep of the house was new to her. When a shelf had to be put up, or the toilet got blocked, she had to take care of it herself.

Goodbye to Old Relationships, Hello to the New

An important part of making a new life is saying goodbye to old relationships and greeting the new ones. You won't be as close to some people, and you might lose all contact with others. It gives you the opportunity to meet new people, and this can pave the way to new friendships. It's also possible to reconnect with old friends with whom you've lost contact over the years. New relationships also give many people a source of emotional and practical support.

Some friends might suddenly not want to have anything to do with you, and vice versa. All these changes are part of creating a new identity.

When Katja wasn't invited to the copper wedding anniversary of one of Kasper's old friends, she was angry at first. Later she felt hurt. After all, she'd got along very well with the friend and his wife. Several other friendships had slipped away too. She felt as if they'd taken sides. On the other hand, she grew closer to a few of her old friends, who had been more on the level of acquaintances. One of them had also recently gotten divorced, and they both profited from the support and understanding they gave each other.

On the Way to Accepting the New

It's difficult for many people to fully accept their new situation. Many find themselves in a more or less constant state of doubt.

The many changes and things to be taken care of following a breakup can be exhausting, and therefore it's natural to wonder if divorce was the right decision. The challenges involved in creating a new identity can simply be too much for some, and at times they can feel very lonely and alone.

Usually doubt is not as big a problem for those who have been left, because the divorce wasn't their decision. More often they have to process painful emotions such as helplessness and betrayal, and they might also long for their ex before they are able to accept the new situation.

If a couple agrees to divorce, and later they both begin to doubt the decision, some choose to give the relationship another shot. Their time apart has given them the opportunity to know themselves better and to see each other in a new light.

At first, both Kasper and Katja occasionally wondered if getting a divorce was the right thing to do. Especially on the days they didn't have the kids, when they thought about all the fun things the other was doing with the children. Both of them felt very alone during these times. One day Kasper walked by Katja's house and couldn't resist peering through the hedge into the kitchen, where Katja was making dinner while both kids sat at the table and drew. He was sad and depressed when he got home, and he decided to not do that again. Nothing good could come of it.

Finding a New Relationship

Some people find someone new before the partnership/marriage ends; some find a new partner soon after the divorce. It takes longer for others. Some prefer living as a single parent, without a partner. Finding a new relationship can be a long process for many people. It can lead to several dilemmas: what type of relationship am I interested in? What about the kids? What should I do if the other person has kids too? Many also doubt if they'll ever manage to find love again and make a relationship work.

On the other hand, lots of divorced parents have a burning wish to find a new partner. This is particularly common when divorce has been on the horizon for some time, when it's been quite a while since they have felt close to their partner. This was the case for Kasper and Katja.

After a while, both Kasper and Katja wanted to find a new partner. They both felt lonely at times; they missed being close and intimate with another person. Katja had second thoughts when she set up a profile on Tinder; it was as if she were doing something wrong. And it felt like a dagger to the heart when she saw that Kasper had a profile, too. Suddenly she was in doubt when she saw his photo – was a divorce the right move to make? Then she thought about all the exhausting fights they'd had over the past two years, and she pushed her doubts away.

PITFALLS

When You are Stuck on One of the Two Paths

The first pitfall in building your new life is getting stuck on the path leading backward. You've fallen into a black hole where you're emotionally overwhelmed by your loss. You can't work up the strength and energy to put your emotions aside and focus on your new life. There can be many reasons for this, and you might need an extra-large oxygen mask, along with support from your network, to move on.

The second pitfall is that you're stuck on the path forward and too quick to dismiss the difficult emotions common after a breakup. It can be a way of protecting yourself from them. And it can lead to distancing yourself too much from your co-parent, even though the problematic emotions are in the background, influencing how you are with your children when they express similar feelings. Avoiding these emotions puts a considerable strain on you, because even though you may look relaxed and balanced on the outside, your nervous system is often acutely active. If you're stuck on this path, it's important to deal with the emotions connected to the past. If it's difficult, seek help and support from your network or from professionals.

QUESTIONS TO ASK YOURSELF

- What has been or is the biggest challenge for you in building a new life after the divorce?

- What was the best thing you got out of the divorce?

- In what situations do you think about whether or not your decision was right? What do you do when this happens?

- How do you take responsibility for making a good life for yourself after the divorce?

CHAPTER 5

Be Adequate Parents, Each in Your Own Way

CENTRAL IDEAS IN THIS CHAPTER

- Be completely divorced.

- Accept your basic situation.

- Act out of your shared love for your children.

- Create a structured, coherent life for your children.

- Help each other to be good parents.

This chapter deals with how divorce radically changes the way you are as parents. It also outlines how important it is to give yourself and each other time and space to get through the divorce, so you can become adequate parents, each in your own way.

I see a lot of parents who navigate a divorce successfully. They build a solid framework, and their children do fine. I also see many who experience challenges, who focus so much on their problems and differences that they overlook their successes and what they have in common – love for their children in particular.

If you've been hit hard emotionally by a divorce, it can be difficult not to tell your children how angry you are at your co-parent. The need is understandable, but at the same time it's important not to air out your frustrations in front of them. Talk to others when this need arises. Remind yourself of what's important: that you and your co-parent raise your children as well as possible.

Be Completely Divorced

Divorce happens on several levels. Legally you and your co-parent are no longer a single entity. One parent may have physical custody and the other visitation rights, with various obligations and rights involved.

The divorce is also physical. You split up with each other and establish two homes, and the children move back and forth between them. You divide your possessions. Things you've shared. Who gets the car, the kitchen table, the sofa, the photo albums of your first years with the kids, etc.?

Divorce is also emotional, and that's particularly challenging for many. It's not something you're going to be done with from one day to the next, and there is no single recipe for how to handle it. Living together several years, having children together, good times, bad times – all these experiences bind us emotionally. In the initial stage of your relationship, when you fall in love, you're bound by intensely positive emotions and fascinated by each other's differences. In time the fascination disappears, and a distancing takes place. You begin to feel frustrated, sometimes by what fascinated you in the beginning. What before was seen as passion and vitality might now be experienced as aggression and self-centeredness. What before seemed to be an easy-going demeanor, a person comfortable in their skin, might now look like apathy, passivity. In the process leading up to a divorce, one or both partners often experience an increasing distance and more negative emotions. Betrayal, anger, pain, disgust, and jealousy are the most common of these emotions.

These negative emotions overwhelm many parents' lives and prevent them from being able to work together well enough with the other parent. To become completely and emotionally divorced is always something you must do alone; your ex can't be a part of it. Of course it's important you show each other understanding for how tough this process is to go through, but again, each partner has to do it on their own.

For some people, the first thing in the morning and the last thing at night they do is think about the divorce. If the breakup goes badly, or if the emotions don't fade away, it can be necessary to seek professional help. Being divorced emotionally is important for you as well as your children, to make sure negative feelings don't stand in the way of collaborating with your co-parent.

Rebekka and Pernilla

Rebekka and Pernilla had been together for ten years and had two children, a four-year-old and an eighteen-month-old, when they divorced. Rebekka was shocked when Pernilla said she wanted a divorce; she felt betrayed because Pernilla had chosen to break up their family after falling in love with someone else. Even though no infidelity was involved, Rebekka felt it was an enormous breach of trust. She was angry that Pernilla wouldn't even try to work out the problems they had. Having two small children together had put a damper on the spontaneity and spirit they'd once had, leaving them with a daily life of routine and household chores they had to maintain.

Rebekka felt they were a close-knit, loving unit, but their family life bored Pernilla. The divorce was a long, drawn-out, and dreadful experience for both of them, which of course affected the children. Their differences had once been a strength, but now they were problems that led to accusations that flew through the air and poisoned the atmosphere between them. Pernilla broke many of their agreements, and Rebekka felt she wasn't living up to her responsibility as a parent, while Pernilla felt that Rebekka was being incredibly rigid about their agreements and working together in general.

Their collaborative relations grew more and more toxic; at times they could barely speak to each other. The exchange days took place at the kids' day care center, with no communication about how the kids had been doing during their time with the other parent.

Accept Your Situation

The Serenity Prayer, which is thought to have been written by the theologian Reinhold Niebuhr, is used in various contexts today. Often it seems relevant when disasters or major disruptions in life take place, when the bedrock of our life shifts. The prayer expresses the wish for "the serenity to accept the things that can't be changed, the courage to change what can be changed, and the wisdom to know the difference." Distinguishing between what we basically can and can't change is central to nearly all circumstances of life, particularly when it comes to divorce.

A fundamental difference between being a couple and being divorced is that when divorced you can't permit yourself to try to change your ex's way of parenting. You have to accept their style, and that can be a tall order, especially if it was a significant reason for the divorce. Totally accepting the person you once chose to have a child with can be absolutely critical for a decent collaboration. You can't change them. You might believe the co-parent's behavior is hurting your child, and of course there are situations that are unacceptable, such as those involving physical or emotional violence. Often, however, we have too negative a picture of our co-parent, because we've seen them as a parent under the emotional stress of living in a difficult relationship.

Another basic condition of divorce is that you're no longer involved in parts of your children's lives. Your children will have many days and experiences without you, and they might also become close to people you don't know particularly well. There will be times when you miss your children when they are with the co-parent, and they will miss you. That's something you can't change, either.

A third basic condition is that even though you strongly disagree with your ex on a lot of things, you have a lot in common – you both love your children, you both want them to have a good childhood and a good life.

During the three years Rebekka and Pernilla were at war with each other, Rebekka became more and more sensitive, with serious stress reactions. One day, when the conflicts had been going on quite a while, she had a talk with a good, supportive friend. Suddenly it became clear to Rebekka that she had to accept that Pernilla was a part of her life, for better or worse, and that Pernilla was who she was. This sudden acceptance made her see she was going to have to find new ways to make her collaboration with Pernilla work. Rebekka stopped fighting against what she perceived as Pernilla's weaknesses and accepted her as the person she was.

As a result of this, their working relationship began functioning better. They both felt they didn't have to be on their guard around each other. Their nervous systems quieted down. Now they could speak openly about how the kids were doing and even listen to each other's perspectives. In time they also began talking about relevant things in their own lives that were difficult, so that each of them was aware of the contours of the children's lives with the other.

Your Shared Love for Your Children

The love you share for your children can be the basis of your working relationship. This also goes for when you disagree with your co-parent and think they are the worst, most egotistical person on the planet, because besides being your irritating ex, they are one of the two most important people in your children's lives. A person to whom the children you share are bonded. As you read these words, imagine your ex as split into two parts: one an ex-partner, the other a parent to your children. It's important to make this distinction. Your ex might well have been a bad partner for you, but that doesn't mean they can't be a decent parent to your children. Weaknesses they might have in some areas of parenting can be counterbalanced by strengths in other areas. If you aren't emotionally divorced yet, this distinction can be particularly difficult to make, because you are outside your emotional window of tolerance (see Chapter 1).

Rebekka and Pernilla sought help both from the district and from taking a course about shared parental custody provided by a state agency.

They both realized how important it was for their kids that the two of them could work together, for the sake of the kids. Though it was difficult, and though there were still plenty of bad feelings between them, this realization helped.

Difference Can be a Strength

Children can handle differences between parents, if parents can do the same. That is, most kids can adapt to various styles of parenting. They can even become more robust from learning to make their way in two different worlds. What they can't handle, however, is too many disagreements and a poisoned atmosphere, a relationship between parents that is basically negative.

Rebekka and Pernilla were very different parents, with different priorities. But they discovered that when they accepted each other's differences as a basic condition, the kids were less anxious. The mood between them was better, and it affected the kids positively, even though they were still getting used to their new reality.

How Do You Talk About Your Ex?

It can be difficult for many people to talk about their co-parent positively. Aspiring to do so means setting a high bar, especially just after a divorce. Children sense it if you say something you don't mean.

When you talk about your co-parent, if you can't be positive, it's fine to keep it neutral. But it means a lot to children to be able to share positive experiences they have with your co-parent, without you showing you can't stand hearing about it.

It can happen that you say something indirectly critical of your ex. "Your mom also hasn't been good at ..." If you don't see eye to eye with your ex on an issue, you could say something like this: "Your mom and I do things in different ways, and that's totally okay." Any concerns about your co-parent's behavior should be dealt with privately, between the two of you, when the children aren't there.

If the children sense that you react very emotionally when they mention your ex, they'll stop doing it quickly, to avoid getting caught in any loyalty conflict. This means they will be on the alert and overly concerned about not making either of their parents angry or unhappy. In Chapter 6, we will hear from Sanne, who puts it well:

"Dad, when you talk bad about Mom, it feels like you're talking bad about me. Mom, when you talk bad about Dad, it feels like you're talking bad about me."

Create Continuity Between the Children's Two Homes

Another thing vital to the children is that you share important information with each other. In other words, that you discuss all kinds of things about your children, whether they are positive, negative, or difficult in some way. By doing so, you ensure that both of you know about any difficulties, plus it gives you someone to discuss important issues or experiences with. You both also gain valuable information about what the children have been doing and experiencing while with their other parent.

You'll have a more nuanced picture of your children's lives, which means you're better able to help and support them when needed. Exchanging this information will also help your children create continuity between their two homes, a difficult task that can rob them of energy they could use doing other things. It's important for children to see their parents talking together and supporting each other when dealing with problems, as well as being pleased about successes.

Rebekka and Pernilla decided they could help the kids adapt by letting them know they were communicating, and that they told each other what they had been doing with the kids during their time together.

Make Each Other Good Parents

Parenthood is teamwork, even when you're divorced. When you're also emotionally divorced, you can help each other become good parents. You know each other's strengths and weaknesses, and you can help and support each other in ways that make you both better parents. You can also "talk each other up" to the children and others around them; in other words, emphasize your ex's parenting strengths and positive sides.

That's a very ambitious project, of course, particularly just after a divorce, but less can help, too. If you can't bring yourself to compliment your ex, the least you can do is not talk about them. Don't push your co-parent's buttons and don't complain about them to others.

Rebekka and Pernilla had finally reached the point where they both felt they were exchanging enough information about the kids. They also talked on the phone when there was something they wanted to discuss about the kids. Not only concerns, but also the good things that happened. Rebekka and Pernilla now saw their differences as an advantage for their kids, and felt they could work together well in bringing up their children. Rebekka found she could even speak highly of Pernilla's new partner, whom she'd accepted and now regarded as an important person in the kids' lives.

A Good Collaborative Atmosphere Gives Strength and Energy

A good atmosphere is an important goal for co-parents. It can make things easier if you try to see everything from the perspective of a helicopter. As you fly over a large area, often you spot systems and connections that are otherwise hidden. The following is a sketch of the positive consequences of helping your ex become a good parent.

When the atmosphere between you speaks of goodwill, your nervous systems become less active, and your windows of emotional tolerance expand. You have more energy to invest in parenting. It's easier for you both to keep your cool in stressful situations, and you become better at accepting and supporting your children. And the better your co-parent does in their life, the more you can trust and respect each other, which in turn motivates you to make each other better parents. A positive circle of collaboration grows out of this and becomes vital to your and your children's quality of life.

The change in climate between Rebekka and Pernilla first came about after they both completely accepted each other and the situation they were in. It changed the dynamic of their collaboration completely, and even though they still disagreed and got annoyed with each other from time to time, they had built up sufficient mutual trust to be able to talk about all major issues. This is how they ensured continuity for their children, who settled into living their lives in two homes. The kids settled down and did well – but only after Rebekka and Pernilla managed to create a good collaborative atmosphere.

PITFALLS

If You Want to Change Each Other

If you become too focused on each other's differences as parents and want to change your co-parent, you risk creating a negative dynamic in your relationship. Often before a divorce you get trapped in a pattern of criticizing each other and demanding that the other change. Some of what you fight about as a couple can carry over into the divorce, at a more intense level.

A type of paradox can come into play. If you accept that you can't change the other person, the possibility of doing so arises. That is, if you accept the basic condition that you can't change this person with whom you have children, and instead focus on changing yourself and how you see your co-parent, your attitude toward them can change. It's possible to start a constructive dialogue with them, allowing the two of you to talk about how best to raise the children. From there on you can affect and be inspired by each other's ways of being a parent.

QUESTIONS TO ASK YOURSELF

- Are you emotionally divorced from your ex?

- How do you create continuity for your child between two homes?

- What would you like for your co-parent to say about you to others?

- What do you say to your children and others when the conversation turns to your co-parent?

- What answer would you like to hear from your children when they grow up, if you were to ask them how you and your co-parent handled your divorce?

BALLOON EXERCISE:

Observe Everything from Above

It's a warm summer day. Not a cloud in the sky, a perfect day to fly in a hot-air balloon.

Imagine you're sitting in the basket as a mild breeze lifts the balloon slowly up over your home. You drift higher and higher, and now you're high enough to see your ex's home as well as your own. You look down and see your children playing outside. They're absorbed in their game. As you sit and watch them, completely relaxed, you can sense their hopes and dreams. Their strengths, their weaknesses. You sense your connection to them, your love for them.

Now you look at your ex's house, at the route your children take between it and your house. You see your ex coming out of the house, and you also see the strong bonds between your children and your ex. You think about all the times you two had together. The bad times and the good times. You also sense what you share. Your children. The love you have for your children.

Then you imagine your children in the future. They're grown up now. You look back on their lives, on what has been good as well as difficult for them. In turn, they look at you and your ex, as their parents. What do they say about the two of you? What would you want them to say?

Now imagine you can see the future from your balloon. There are several paths you and your co-parent can take. Some paths lead to difficult places for your children, others lead to places from where your children will speak in glowing terms about their childhood.

Look down at your house and see your children playing. Feel your love for them, feel how you together with your co-parent are creating their childhoods and their futures.

CHAPTER 6

Give Your Children What They Need

CENTRAL IDEAS IN THIS CHAPTER

- Support your children emotionally.

- Allow your child to get support from other adults or children.

- Be curious about your child's behavior.

- Help your children handle the new circumstances in their lives.

- Show your children there is hope.

This chapter has been influenced by knowledge of how children react to divorce, as expressed by Øyvind Øvreeide (2009), and used in courses at the Center for Family Development that deal with shared parental responsibility. A good divorce is all about

giving your children what they need. Most children make it through a divorce just fine, but as is the case for parents, a divorce is a major upheaval in their lives that requires extra care and support. Part of what children are very focused on is how each of their parents tackles the divorce.

Children Don't Want Conflict

Children need their parents to get along. From my many conversations with children whose parents are going through a difficult breakup, I know the last thing children want is to make the situation worse. Their greatest wish is for their mother and father to be okay with each other, and very small children often want their parents to get back together. As they grow older, they understand that's not an option, just as they can see that it's not always desirable. But they always want very much for their parents to get along.

Children's nervous systems need peace, security, and predictability. When they sense their parents are more or less okay by themselves as well as with people they have to cooperate with as parents, children can focus on their own lives and on growing up. On exploring the world around them and returning to their base of security – their parents. This goes not only for children living with divorced parents, but for all children. Conflicts are okay, and it's also okay to express emotions, as long as children see their parents are able to calm themselves down and that the mood between them is positive most of the time.

Children Form Their Own Understanding

With the best of intentions, many parents protect their children by not telling them much about what's going on. If they get into a lot of arguments before the divorce, and the children overhear the fighting, the children might think it's about them, that they've done something wrong. They might then feel it's their fault that their parents are divorcing. Children need emotional support to adapt to their new circumstances and understand that the divorce has nothing to do with them. It can also be necessary later on, even after you've established a good working relationship with your ex, to tell the children repeatedly, to get the message through: it's not their fault.

Support Your Children Emotionally

Often during a divorce, children experience complex and contradictory emotions they can't explain. They might be relieved that their parents don't argue anymore, and that as a result there's a better atmosphere when they're with only one of them, yet they can miss the parent they aren't with. They can also be angry with the parent who decided to get the divorce. Maybe because their other parent feels terrible about it, and they might feel sorry for that parent, and might feel it's their job to take care of them. They can also be angry at their father's or mother's new partner, for destroying their dream of their parents getting back together. Or maybe they feel guilty about liking the new partner and thus feel they're being disloyal to the other parent.

Most children can't come close to expressing these conflicting emotions, so they show them in other ways. Often they need help from others to make sense of them. When the emotions take up much of their inner lives, it can feel like a restlessness inside that they try to deal with in various ways. It's not unusual to see children regress to an earlier stage of development, where suddenly they need help to do basic things they had no trouble doing before.

When your children can't understand or explain their emotions, it can help them tremendously if you put into words various descriptions of how they might be feeling, and then tell them it's normal and understandable to feel that way. This mirroring of your children's emotional state can lead them to understand themselves and their situation.

This can be difficult to do if you're in a crisis and barely able to handle your own emotions. When you're overwhelmed by what you're feeling, it's almost impossible to have a clear sense of how your children are doing and thus mirror their emotions. And that's also why it's very important to take care of yourself – see Chapter 3 – so you're able to help your children this way.

For many children, the divorce can lead to a temporary identity crisis. They have to adjust to their new lives as children of divorced parents, to all the new routines, exchange days, having two homes and perhaps new step-parents, step-sisters, and step-brothers. That's a challenge they didn't choose to face, and like adults, they need time and space to get comfortable with everything. Children are also often affected by the myths as well as true stories told about divorce; they've seen their friends' and perhaps their friends' parents' ways of tackling the problems of divorce. It's vital for them to find their own identity as children of divorced parents, and they have to adapt to and create stability and cohesion when living in two homes. This is a major challenge, and it can lead to anger, disappointment, and despair.

Allow Your Children to Get Support from Others

In this situation, having a network is very important for children. Being particularly close to some other adults, such as grandparents, neighbors, day care teachers, or school teachers, can be a great support for children, especially when their parents are under extra pressure. Many schools also have student groups for children of divorced parents, which provide a good opportunity to talk about their emotions and discover they're not the only ones who feel the way they do. The Danish Ngo, Center for Family Development, has developed a type of children's group they call "Shared Children – Whole Children" that many schools sponsor. It has helped children who have problems after their parents' divorce.

Look at the Child's Behavior

Children behave in various ways when they're put in a situation where they have to develop emotionally. The differences are partly due to their ages and personalities, but another important factor is how much time and energy each parent has for the child, in addition to the atmosphere of the parents' collaboration. Children's ways of handling a divorce depend on the inner and outer resources available to them and how big a challenge the divorce is.

Therefore, the child's reactions can be seen as a completely understandable way of tackling their situation, given their resources. That's why it's important for parents and other caregivers to find out what's behind the child's behavior.

Their reactions may also differ in their two homes, which is why it's necessary for co-parents to talk about these reactions, so they can support each other and the child while they're all in a period of upheaval.

Show You Can Handle the New Circumstances of Your Life

When your children sense you can handle the major disruptions life brings, they feel safe. The better you take care of yourself, the easier it is to be there for your children and handle your new circumstances. It's totally okay that they see you being emotional. They will sense it anyway. What's important is that you tell them what you're going through. You can say it in a way appropriate to their ages, so they understand that emotions are okay. When the children see their parents putting on the oxygen masks and handling difficult situations, they learn to take care of themselves when the need arises.

Support Your Children in Handling the New Circumstances in Their Lives

Children may also need specific support in dealing with their new circumstances. For example, they might need help with how to talk about the divorce with their friends and at school. They have to learn a new rhythm, learn how to live in two places and all that goes with it, a new way of doing things in daily life. It can also help children to take something along on exchange days, such as a teddy bear or a favorite sweatshirt, that gives them a sense of connection to both their homes. Children need grown-ups' support in forming mental and emotional continuity between the two worlds. It's an enormous strain for them to deal with this alone.

Malte, Nadja, and Sanne

Malte is five years old and goes to day care. He's an only child. Nadja is ten years old and has a four-year-old brother. Sanne is fourteen and is also an only child.

The three of them have something in common: their parents are divorced. They don't know each other, but the stories of how they react to the divorces will unfold over the following pages. Through their behavior, they try in various ways to make grown-ups understand what's going on inside them. This is true for all children, not only those with divorced parents.

Day Care Child – When a Night Diaper was Needed Again, the Parents Sought Help

When children don't want to worsen an already malfunctioning collaboration, they come up with various strategies to handle the stress and anxiety it causes. Either they react internally by suppressing their own needs or trying to make themselves invisible, or they start misbehaving. Often the children who react internally are overlooked because they seem to adapt well, while the ones who cause problems are often misunderstood, because their behavior isn't recognized as an expression of their inner pain, caused by their difficult circumstances.

Five-year-old Malte didn't understand at first what it meant when his mother and father got divorced. He knew there were fewer arguments at home, and he sensed that he was less physically tense. His parents agreed on joint custody, and that was hard for Malte to get used to. He missed his father when he was with his mother, and vice versa. Often at bedtime he had a stomach ache and needed more physical contact. He'd stopped needing a night diaper when he was four, but now he started wetting the bed again. The teachers in his day care center noticed a change in his behavior. He had sudden bouts of rage, and it was difficult to get him to settle down, even for his favorite adult at the center.

Malte's parents had an asynchronous breakup: his mother had found a new partner, and his father was very hurt and unhappy and overwhelmed by the split. He was also mad at Malte's mother, and wanted as little to do with her as possible.

Malte's mother got over the breakup quickly, and she couldn't understand why Malte's father was still reacting so strongly a year later. They still didn't talk much on exchange days about how Malte's week had been. Finally Malte's behavior became so worrying that the day care center called his parents in for a meeting. At first both of them were sorry to hear that he wasn't doing well, but soon they began arguing and blaming each other for his problems.

After the meeting, a district family center began helping them with their problematic breakup. They also learned how to spot what lay behind Malte's behavior, in order to better support him emotionally. His father and mother simply needed to cooperate better, to make sure he didn't have to create continuity between his two lives all by himself.

School Child - Anger and Silence, a Cry for Help

Nadja was ten years old and in fourth grade. She had two younger siblings, both of whom were in day care. Nadja was an outgoing girl, with many good friends in her class. After her parents divorced, most of the time she lived with her mother – nine days out of every two weeks. Nadja began behaving differently in school. She had seldom been involved in conflicts before, but now during recess she often clashed with other girls, sometimes even with boys. It finally got to the point where most of the girls didn't want to play with her.

Both of her parents felt she was quieter at home, and when they asked her how she was doing, she answered lightly, "I'm fine." She spent most of her time in her room on her phone. Nadja's parents had disagreed strongly about where she and her younger siblings should live the majority of the time, and it ended with a judge making the decision for them. After this, her parents seldom spoke to each other, and the atmosphere on exchange days was chilly, to say the least.

Her father and mother were both worried about Nadja, especially when they were called in for a meeting at her school about her change in behavior. They were told about the school's support group for children of divorced parents, and that she could talk to her class teacher if she needed to, which her parents thought was a good idea. In the support group, Nadja talked about how horrible she felt because her parents hardly spoke to each other at all, to the extent that she felt they hated each other. In many ways it was easier when they argued. After the support group had been meeting for some time, the parents were called in; the children had some things they wanted to say to them. Nadja's parents were moved by what the children said, and afterward they decided to seek help to improve the atmosphere in their collaboration. By the time the support group ended, Nadja was better able to communicate how she was feeling, and when she felt bad, she talked with her class teacher. The support group also got together on their own initiative once in a while during recess, to talk or just to play.

Nadja's anger and behavior in school can be seen as a cry for help, as evidence that she and her parents needed help and support. Her silence at home can likewise be seen as her way of not making the bad vibes between her parents any worse.

Teenager's Distance to Her Parents, Caused by Helplessness

Sanne was fourteen and in eighth grade. She was an only child. When she was thirteen, she'd chosen to live the majority of the time with her father. She'd contacted the authorities herself to change the custody agreement, by which she'd split her time equally between her parents. They had divorced five years earlier. For the first two years it was almost as if they weren't divorced, because her father ate with them once a week, and they often took vacations together. When her mother found a new partner, "all hell broke loose." Her father no longer ate with them, and suddenly the atmosphere between her parents was tense. Her mother moved in with her new partner, who had two kids, both younger than Sanne. She felt uncomfortable and under pressure when she lived with her mother. The house was big enough, but her mother wasn't as close to her or as much there for her as before. Also, her mother suddenly felt her father wasn't a particularly good father, that much of what he did was wrong; she felt he gave in to Sanne too much and was too permissive.

Her father was mad at her mother, too, and said bad things about her. Sanne's mother didn't want her to go with her father on a three-week vacation to Thailand, because it interfered with her own plans. At first Sanne tried to mediate between them, but finally she got so sick of it that she gave up. She pulled away from her parents and started hang-ing out with a group of ninth-grade boys and girls who stayed out late and drank beer. Often she got home late at night and broke the rules she and her parents had agreed on. Her mother was worried about the change in Sanne, and she contacted her ex, who at first made light of her concerns. He claimed Sanne was just being a normal teenager. They were both worried, however, that Sanne was shutting them out of her life, and finally it reached the point where they were afraid she was getting herself into a bad situation. They set up a meeting with the school psychologist so they could all talk together. During the meeting, it came out that the conflict between Sanne's parents was a problem for her. She was unhappy, and tired of hearing them put each other down. It was affecting her physically. She'd mostly lost hope that her parents would ever get along better. She also said that when she was with her new friends, she didn't think about her mother and father, a welcome relief, but still, somewhere inside she felt helpless and lonely.

Show Your Children It's Going To Be Okay Again

Children can handle a lot, and for a period of time they can set aside their own needs if their parents are in a crisis. If the situation becomes permanent, however, something called "learned helplessness" occurs. The term refers to how children learn from their experiences that they can't change a situation or problem, no matter how hard they try.

Sanne had almost given up. She couldn't see any way she could do more. But fortunately, her parents didn't just ignore their worries about her. They realized what was causing Sanne to act the way she did. Speaking with the school psychologist led them to resolve their differences with-out involving their daughter. It wasn't easy, by any means, and it took quite a while for them   to get along better. They also began spending more time with Sanne, listening to what was important to her, what she was involved in. At first Sanne still acted standoffish toward them, but she was happy they were paying attention to her. Slowly she regained her trust in both her parents.

PITFALLS

When They're Needed Most, Parents Are Often in Crisis

Right after a divorce, parents are often under great emotional pressure, trying to find a foothold in their new circumstances. Their children are also experiencing a lot of stress. Not only are they trying to make sense of their own emotional reactions, but they also have to adjust to the practical and physical realities of new homes and new routines that may include a change of school, as well as new partners their father or mother may have (along with the partners' own children). Their need for attention, care and support is much greater than normal, at a time when their parents are busy handling their own emotional reactions to the breakup and creating their own framework for a new life. This is why many children feel left to themselves after a divorce. If their parents' breakup is difficult, children often react by suppressing their own needs, which may result in the adults around them overlooking the children's needs. Most children can handle a short period of turbulence and crisis, as long as it's not permanent. It's essential that you as a parent navigate your divorce well so you can quickly support your children.

FACTS ABOUT EMOTIONAL MIRRORING

Emotional mirroring involves an adult verbally expressing a child's emotional state. We see and sense that a child feels bad, and we might say something like: "You look sad today." And we might ask what the child needs. Maybe give them a hug. This type of emotional mirroring is important to children, because it helps to calm their nervous system. It's important for children to feel they're being noticed and understood, and that it's okay to feel the way they do. This is how children sense that they understand themselves. And when they experience this emotional mirroring many times – maybe not every time they are upset, but often – they will be better able to accept their emotions and calm down when no adults are around to comfort them. Research has shown that for most children, being met with emotional mirroring as few as one out of three times in relevant situations is sufficient (Circle Of Security, 2013).

Many of us can't stand seeing our children unhappy or angry, and we're too quick to give them good advice to make the feeling go away. It's not wrong to help your child, but you need to take a step back and watch the child, just as the child needs to know you see how they feel, before offering your advice.

When we – both children and adults – experience intense and difficult emotions, it's hard to think clearly and therefore be in a position to take good advice. That can only happen when you feel understood and in a more settled state.

Think back to a crisis you've experienced, where you were emotionally upset. How did you want the people around you to react? Were you able to heed their advice? Or did you need them to just be with you a while, to sense how you were doing before advising you?

QUESTIONS TO ASK YOURSELF

- How have your children reacted to your divorce?
- Are you overlooking anything in your children's behavior?
- Are you misunderstanding anything about your children's behavior?
- Is there anyone your children can speak to besides you and your co-parent about how they are feeling?
- How do you communicate with your co-parent about your children's behavior and reactions?

CHAPTER 7

Get Support From Your Network

CENTRAL IDEAS IN THIS CHAPTER

- A network often provides protection.

- A network is important when parents have problems working together.

- A network can ease conflicts, but it can also worsen them.

This chapter deals with the important role your network plays for you, your co-parent, and your children. Your network is your friends and family and other important people in your family's life, such as neighbors, co-workers, your children's teachers, and the parents of your children's friends. A network is important for children; contact with other adults who know them can be a vital source of support. A network can help keep conflicts from growing, but it also has the potential to do the opposite.

The Protective Role of a Network

Research in divorce points to a family's network as being a protective factor. A large group that includes grandparents, uncles, aunts, step-parents, siblings, and children and adults in day care centers, schools, and clubs can in various ways play an important role for adults as well as children in their daily lives.

The Important Role of Grandparents

In particular, a good, stable contact with grandparents is important; in most cases they not only have a close relationship with their grandchildren, but enough room in their lives to accommodate the children's emotions. When you ask grandparents about their grandchildren, many of them say it's much easier being grandparents than parents, because you don't have the primary responsibility for them. You can support the family and simply enjoy watching your grandchildren grow up and mature. Many grandparents also have more time to do things with children than when they were the parents of small children.

Timeout with Grandparents

Many children's relationship with their grandparents is uncomplicated, too, and being with their grandparents can feel like a much-needed timeout from a busy life. Grandparents can also step in and relieve parents who need a pause in their lives, to gather the strength and energy necessary for being a parent and working together with a co-parent. To make their oxygen masks, in other words.

Not all children have a close relationship with their grandparents, however. Some grandparents live far away, some may be sick or even dead, and some simply don't have a stable and heartening relationship with their grandchildren, the type that can contribute positively to a family's everyday life. In such cases, there might be other people who can help, if you and your children trust them.

Support from Good Friends or Neighbors

Friendships are important to many people, because friends can give them emotional support. Some are also lucky enough to have good neighbors who can lend a hand and be of practical support when needed. You can share meals with neighbors, for example, or shop for each other, or look after each other's children. The better you as a parent are at asking for help and support from your network, the easier it will be to get through the really tough times. You'll also be sending an important signal to your children, that you're not afraid to ask for help and support when it's needed.

A Network Can Ease Conflicts

A network can contribute in many ways to a decent collaborative atmosphere between co-parents by easing a looming conflict. There are times when a network can be a deciding factor as to whether or not a conflict between co-parents gets resolved. This is the case in the following story.

Iben and Frank

Iben and Frank split up after fifteen years of married life. They had grown apart from each other and had agreed on a divorce, although Iben had been the one to make the decision. Their children, fifteen-year-old Otto and thirteen-year-old Andreas, were unhappy about the divorce at first. But when Iben and Frank seemed okay with their decision, the two boys quickly adjusted. Before long, Iben found someone new. It was a shock to Frank; he wasn't at all ready for a new relationship. Iben moved in with her new partner soon after, and when she wanted to introduce him to the boys, the situation deteriorated. Frank gave Iben the cold shoulder and bad-mouthed her and her new partner to the boys.

When the boys saw that Frank was hurt and angry, they felt they had to take his side. Frank also spoke badly about Iben to neighbors and some of their old mutual friends. When Iben heard about it, she got mad at Frank and began speaking the same way about him to her network. Iben's father ended up playing an important role. He spent a lot of time calming her down, and he tried to get her to see what drove Frank to act the way he did. Fortunately, Frank had a very good relationship with Iben's father, who took the initiative to talk to Frank about what was going on. He showed Frank that he understood his difficult situation. The two men took several walks in the nearby forest, and eventually Frank also cooled off and began to accept that Iben had found someone else and was living with him. When Frank became less emotional, the boys followed suit. Frank made it a point to show his network that things were going better, and he stopped speaking badly about Iben to his neighbors.

A Network Can Worsen a Conflict

Of course, not every member of a network contributes directly to lowering the temperature of a conflict as Iben's father did. It's extremely challenging when a parent sees their adult child get hurt and turn into an emotional wreck. It's hard for them when their child's partner, the father/mother of their grandchild, doesn't treat their child well. The following story illustrates this.

Peter and Tina

Peter and Tina had been together for five years. They were the parents of six-month-old Sara. Their marriage had always been rocky; in fact, they'd had Sara as an attempt to help their relationship. But it didn't work. Peter couldn't stand being with Tina, because in his view she turned hysterical when she didn't get enough sleep from nursing Sara at night. When he suggested starting Sara on a bottle, Tina rejected the idea; nursing was much better for their baby, she said, and he really should try to understand that she had way too much on her plate, that she needed him to do more of the housework, shopping, etc. Peter gradually got fed up and at last decided to move out. Tina was hurt terribly, especially because Peter's leaving put her in a very tight spot. It infuriated her. She felt he shouldn't be allowed to see Sara, given that he wasn't willing to take on an important part of parental responsibility. After several months of being cut off from his daughter, he contacted the social authorities. In the meantime, Tina's mother had stepped in and taken care of many of the practical things having to do with Sara.

Tina brought her mother along to the meeting with the authorities. She seemed even angrier at Peter than Tina was; during the meeting she sat and stared at him, which poisoned the atmosphere and led to several interruptions. Tina occasionally opened up, but Tina's mother repeatedly emphasized Peter's complete lack of responsibility. This made any resolution impossible, and the meeting ended as a total disaster. As a consequence, Tina and Peter were offered conflict resolution mediation.

At the mediation meeting, with only Tina, Peter, and a negotiator present, the couple agreed to a gradual increase in the time Peter could spend with his daughter. Both of them were satisfied when the meeting ended. But when Tina came home and told her mother about the agreement, her mother got mad at her. She went on and on about Peter's irresponsibility and claimed the agreement was doomed from the start. Doubts grew in Tina's mind. She was split between her mother and Peter, which affected her as Peter began seeing Sara. It led to small conflicts. Tina felt stressed, under pressure.

In other words, Tina's mother poured gasoline on the fire that others were trying to put out. It made the whole process difficult, of course, and it hindered both Tina and Peter in their attempt to establish a collaboration with visitation rights.

PITFALLS

When Family or Friends Get Too Involved

From Tina's mother's perspective, what she did made perfect sense. Seeing her daughter so unhappy and under serious pressure made her feel terrible. In her eyes Peter had betrayed both Tina and Sara, and when someone abandoned a child so early in the child's life, she felt they gave up the right to see the child. Tina's mother was very upset; it was all she could do to calm herself down. That's why it was so difficult for her to see the situation in the light of what was best for Sara and Tina. Her behavior placed

Tina in a dilemma: should she listen to her mother, or to herself and what she learned during the conflict resolution process?

Research tells us that a conflict in a divorce can become deadlocked when a network resists cooperation between parents. This is why experts in difficult conflicts involve networks when working with a family to establish to a well-functioning collaboration (Lawick, 2015).

When you are close to a family involved in a divorce, it's important to look critically at yourself and your participation – are you contributing to resolving conflicts by what you say and do, or perhaps unwittingly maintaining or even worsening them? And are you yourself, as part of the network, being harmed by your long-term involvement? If you are, it's important to find ways to keep your cool.

If you as a parent feel the network surrounding your children is hindering your collaboration with your co-parent, it might be a good idea to ask for professional help to set up a meeting for everyone involved.

QUESTIONS TO ASK YOURSELF

- How do you get support from your network?
- How do your children get support from the network?
- Does your network contribute to a fruitful collaboration?

QUESTIONS FOR YOUR NETWORK

- How can you support the family without escalating the conflicts?

- How can you contribute to a better collaboration between the parents that helps the children?

- How can you seek help and support if you are emotionally affected by the parents' conflict?

Good Advice:

Find Someone in Your Network Who Can Support You Emotionally

Find someone in your network who will listen to and understand you, when you tell them how your divorce has affected you. Hopefully, you can even talk to them about your intense, negative emotions concerning your co-parent.

It needs to be someone who won't be influenced by what you tell them, who won't turn around and demonize your co-parent.

CHAPTER 8

Seek Help When It Becomes Difficult to Cooperate

This chapter has been greatly influenced by developmental research done at the Center for Family Development, which I took part in. It deals with what you and your ex can do when stuck in a difficult spot in your collaboration, how you both can change your negative interactions to get back on track. It's normal that the time immediately following a breakup is demanding and

extremely emotional, but difficulties in working together can occur at any time.

What characterizes serious and long, drawn-out conflicts in a divorce is that the two people involved are possibly more closely bound than ever before, possibly more than they will ever admit to being. Their thoughts center on each other. In a nutshell, a piece of paper might say they are divorced, but in a sense they've never been more married, given the extent to which they are emotionally tied to each other. Not in any beneficial way, of course; their feelings and thoughts about each other are strenuous and negative, not loving.

Working together as co-parents can be hard. At first everything might go well, with the best of intentions to remain good friends, but it can be difficult to maintain a good relationship for many reasons, especially when changing visitation rights or the children's schools or day care centers, or when one parent finds a new partner. Emotions and these new circumstances can interfere. (See Chapter 2.)

External factors may also put a lot of pressure on an ex-couple's nervous systems, limiting their ability to handle painful emotions and sparking a negative dynamic in their relations.

If a conflict is allowed to develop, suddenly it can move to a level where it's difficult to resolve. The following story illustrates such a situation.

Mathilde and Carsten

Mathilde and Carsten had three children, eleven-year-old Anton, eight-year-old Nikoline, and five-year-old Noor. They had been together for twelve years, and for some time they hadn't been getting along particularly well; they had become more like two co-workers than a married couple. The calm, steady man Mathilde had fallen for wasn't attractive anymore. She felt Carsten lacked initiative and was boring, and she let him know that frequently. Out of frustration, she had an affair with Carsten's best friend, Jesper.

Carsten had fallen for Mathilde's vivaciousness, spontaneity, and direct manner, but later on in their relationship, these qualities became too much for him. She always seemed dissatisfied, and he retreated to his workshop whenever she criticized him.

They grew further and further apart. It was a vicious circle; she became even more critical of him, and he withdrew further and avoided her.

Demonizing the Other

After Carsten and Mathilde got divorced, when they talked to their network about how they were getting along, they both said something like, "We don't argue about anything, because we don't talk to each other." Their relations were icy, and it was clear to everyone that just because they weren't talking didn't mean there were no conflicts. On the contrary, their problems had become so serious that they'd given up any semblance of dialogue. Their children sensed this, and it severely affected them.

A conflict (see figure, page 100) always builds up over time, unless it is resolved quickly. It starts with a disagreement about something, and soon it's not possible to separate the problem from your co-parent. You begin to doubt each other's good intentions. Often you tell your side of the story to your network, and often the network is supportive and validates your version, which only serves to maintain the level of conflict. If the conflict becomes more serious, you eventually stop speaking to your co-parent altogether. And when that happens, your imagination runs wild. You focus on your ex's negative qualities and forget the positives; you begin to demonize them. Once you've created a very one-sided and unfavorable picture of them, you've given yourself permission to expand the conflict. You're at a place where it's difficult to find a path back to agreement and collaboration. *As we will see later on, Carsten and Mathilde disagreed on where the children should live, and their time in court with each other escalated the conflict even further.*

Resistance to Seeking Help

When you've heightened the conflict and given up on dialogue, you've also assigned the guilt to your ex. You don't want to be around them, and therefore you don't want to seek help as a couple to solve or at least ease the conflict. Maybe you've given up all hope that your ex will change the least bit, and often you don't see yourself as needing to change in any way. Even though there's no physical contact with them, your nervous system is still highly activated, as you're often thinking about them.

For quite a while, neither Carsten nor Mathilde thought they needed to seek help, because they each felt the other was the cause of the problem. The conflict grew, as did their anger with each other.

Shed Light on the Negative Interaction

To understand how Mathilde and Carsten's conflict developed, we need to look at what was going on in their married life. Like many couples, without being aware of it they had become trapped in a pattern of behavior known as fight-or-flight. One fights and the other flees. The fighter's weapon is often words and criticism, while the one who flees retreats from the situation. This fight-or-flight pattern creates a spiral of frustration and distance when a couple gets caught in it (Johnson, 2015).

Mathilde missed the sense of intimacy and attention in her life, which is why she criticized Carsten. When he didn't confirm or hold her, she felt inadequate and unloved. Carsten got angry when Mathilde criticized him, and he also felt inadequate because of all the things she wanted, all her demands. The more she criticized him, the colder he felt inside and the more time he spent out in his workshop.

They were caught in a negative pattern. They grew further and further apart, becoming more frustrated and lonely all the time. Mathilde felt Carsten's workshop was more important to him than she was.

The few times Carsten spoke with other people about the conflict, he told them how unfair Mathilde was, how difficult it was to satisfy her. When Mathilde spoke to her girlfriends, she characterized Carsten as an extremely boring and passive man she didn't care about much anymore.

Carsten and Mathilde accused each other of being the reason why they weren't getting along. Their distance and frustration only worsened, and they couldn't spot the negative pattern of interplay they were caught in.

Carsten finally found out that Mathilde and Jesper were having an affair, and it enraged and hurt him badly. He wanted a divorce immediately.

Mathilde agreed that they should get divorced, the sooner the better. She ended her affair with Jesper and moved into a house not far away from the family home. Carsten kept the house. They couldn't agree on visitation rights, however. Carsten felt she should only be a weekend mother, because her behavior had shown she wasn't to be trusted. He didn't want their children to be influenced by her values. Mathilde, on the other hand, believed Carsten had been just as terrible a father as he had been a partner to her; therefore she felt he was the one who should be limited to weekends with the kids.

Mathilde and Carsten both hoped the divorce would solve their problems, but it turned out that what had been hard for them to deal with as a couple became even harder after the divorce.

They stopped speaking altogether and tried to solve their disagreements about the children through the social authorities, but they couldn't settle on which of them should have primary physical custody. It ended up in court.

On the day the case was to be heard, Carsten didn't show up. He had forgotten the date, and Mathilde was furious. The hearing was postponed, and a new date was set. At the hearing, each of them talked about the other's weaknesses and their own strengths as a parent. They each painted the other black and themselves white.

The court ruled that the two youngest should live with Mathilde and the oldest with Carsten. After negotiations about visitation rights, they decided that all three children should live with each of them a week at a time. But even though they had an agreement, the conflict wasn't solved. Carsten was angry and hurt about what Mathilde had said about him at the hearing, and he wanted as little communication with her as possible. Mathilde was angry too, and she was frustrated that Carsten didn't answer her emails. In addition, he had explained to the kids in detail why the divorce was all her fault.

Mathilde and Carsten's negative pattern of interaction held them in its grip. And the problems it caused the kids kept getting worse.

Years passed with no change in the situation. The first thing in the morning and the last thing at night Mathilde thought about was Carsten. How much she hated him, how completely he'd failed both her and the kids. Twice Carsten had postponed their exchange day for twenty-four hours; the second time she had to cancel a night out with some friends.

She suspected him of postponing just to spite her. If only he would just get over it, she thought. She could understand that her affair with his best friend had upset and hurt him, but five years was a long time to hold it against her!

Take Responsibility for Your Part

Mathilde and Carsten had another hearing in court a few years later. Carsten wanted primary physical custody of the two youngest and sole custody of all three children. The problems Mathilde and Carsten had cooperating with each other were an enormous burden on both of them. The judge and their lawyers decided to give Carsten and Mathilde the option of going through couples therapy for divorced parents before the court made a decision.

They chose to do the therapy, where they began dealing with their negative pattern of communication and behavior. It was hard for them, because they were both deeply invested in blaming each other for what had happened and for why their kids weren't doing well.

Mathilde and Carsten worked on seeing things from the other's point of view and listening to what the other said. The listening part was very difficult, because they both had answers ready for what they thought the other was going to say. But after several sessions they began to hear each other.

They realized how much their lack of cooperation had weighed them down. Mathilde began to see that when she'd criticized Carsten, he'd felt inadequate and desperate, which was why he had retreated from their relationship. And Carsten understood that his passive anger and distance had in turn angered and frustrated Mathilde. During the therapy they also realized that when they were focused on their negative feelings toward the other they almost forgot about the children's well-being. When the therapy began focusing on their collaboration, the therapist asked them a question: what do you think your kids would say if they were asked as grown-ups how their parents had handled getting divorced? They looked at each other, and Mathilde said, "We have to change how we're treating each other." Carsten nodded.

The shift from blaming your ex for the problem to seeing and accepting your share of the responsibility for your problems with your ex in parenting can be uncomfortable and difficult. And accepting someone you don't get along with can be very challenging. But being partly responsible also gives you a chance to change a pattern of interaction; potentially it gives both of you the hope and energy to improve your climate of collaboration.

Carsten and Mathilde each began to see their own role in the problems with their collaboration. They became aware of what set off the negative pattern, and they stopped pushing each other's buttons. When they got back to discussing things concerning their children, Mathilde didn't verbally attack Carsten, and he expressed more clearly what he was thinking and how he was feeling. This improved their communication, and as time went by, they formed a better collaboration.

Look Behind the Other Person's Behavior

When Mathilde and Carsten realized they were trapped in a negative pattern, and their behavior was based on hurt feelings and attempts to protect themselves, they slowly began to accept each other. When Carsten withdrew, Mathilde now understood that he was shielding himself from some very distressing emotions. He was also terrified of losing contact with his children, which frayed his nerves even more. But when Mathilde didn't criticize him, Carsten understood that Mathilde had no interest at all in cutting him off from the kids; therefore he dared to be more open and generous. He also realized that distancing himself affected Mathilde. She felt very much alone with the responsibility of raising the children, because she needed to discuss things with him. Gradually he realized that criticizing him was her way of protecting herself as well as expressing her frustration with his passive attitude and withdrawal, which she interpreted as him simply not being interested in the kids and her. Her affair with Jesper was in fact an attempt to get his attention.

When It Gets Very Difficult – Prolonged Adultery

Mathilde and Carsten's story deals with adultery, which was a painful development and made working together even more difficult in the beginning. Carsten found out about the affair quickly, however, and Mathilde broke it off.

There's much more at stake with a prolonged affair. A fundamental bond of trust with someone you have been very close to has been broken. They have lied to you and lived a double life over a significant period of time, so how can you trust such a person?

For some people, the betrayal and pain are so severe that it's enormously difficult to have anything other than a remote collaboration. It may be hard for others to understand that someone who was cheated on for a long time can't let it go, even after several years. But there's a good reason for this. When you're close to another person, and perhaps have been in a happy, secure relationship, the pain and betrayal cuts much deeper. The situation is fundamentally different than if both parties are generally dissatisfied with the relationship and emotionally distant from each other.

Many people find it necessary to seek professional help to deal with the betrayal. Taking care of yourself this way can recharge your batteries, perhaps to the extent that your collaboration with your co-parent looks okay to your children.

PITFALLS

When Your Children's Problems Worsen the Conflicts

A pattern I often come across in complicated divorces is an unfortunate dynamic that heightens the conflict between parents. It arises out of love for a child and the pain a parent experiences when the child isn't doing well. Intense emotions almost always emerge in difficult divorces. Often one parent leaves the relationship, while the other parent is abandoned. Adultery may have been hidden for a long period of time, perhaps discovered by accident. Such a breach of trust between parents creates distance, and communication and collaboration are at a minimum. The atmosphere between them is icy, and they don't speak with each other on exchange days. Both of them are in fact good parents. They're different, but they are there for the children emotionally, and they're active and loving parents. The children do just fine while staying with each parent, but the parents don't know that, because they're not speaking. The children protect themselves by not talking about their experiences with the other parent, because they can clearly see how their father gets angry and upset when he talks about their mother, how their mother changes the subject when their father's name is mentioned. What the children want most of all is for their parents to be good friends. They don't tell anyone, though; they don't share their troubling emotions. This is how they shield themselves from the situation they dread the most, exchange day, when their parents are cold to each other. They react when they get to their rooms; they're sullen, they throw things around in anger or get a stomach ache and cry. They might also experience anxiety.

The parent who picks the children up on exchange day assumes they've been like this the entire time they've been with the co-parent, which of course means that the co-parent is a bad parent – presumably just as bad as they were a partner. And the same thing happens on the next exchange day, with the other parent. The process escalates, and the parents blame each other for how badly the children are doing. The more the accusations fly through the air, the worse the children feel, though in fact they get along just fine with both parents. But the children are hampered by their parents' anger with each other. The children shield themselves from their longing for their parents to get along by not talking about this wish. Many deadlocked and unhappy divorces have this pattern. The best intentions to protect children intensify the conflict between parents when they accuse each other of causing their children's problems.

QUESTIONS TO ASK YOURSELF

- How do you protect yourself when you're under emotional pressure?

- Have you ever been caught in a negative pattern of interaction?

- What part do you play in this pattern you and your co-parent find yourselves in?

- What do you do about it?

- Are you in a place where you need help to get back on track in working together?

The Staircase of Conflict

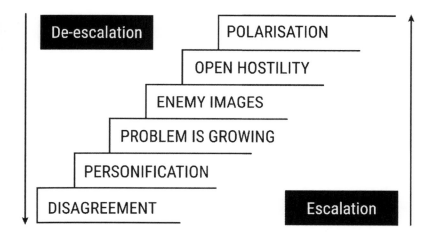

The Stairway of Conflict illustrates how conflicts can grow from disagreements into polarizing enemy images of each other. It also shows that it's possible to descend the stairway by talking and reaching agreements. It's important to remember that disagreements are completely normal and healthy, but problems arise if you don't deal with them in a healthy way.

CHAPTER 9

Maintain a Good Working Relationship

CENTRAL IDEAS IN THIS CHAPTER

- Visitation rights can be changed.

- Diversity is a strength.

- You can't change the past.

- Everyone wins when there is a good atmosphere in a collaboration.

This chapter is about how parents can make agreements that help them focus on their collaboration, and how they can remain good co-parents as they work together.

The story about Max and Naja illustrates how several mutual acknowledgments and subsequent agreements helped get them back on track when their collaboration faced challenges.

Max and Naja

Max and Naja were the parents of eleven-year-old Tim and three-year-old Axel. They both had gone through a difficult period right after their divorce two years earlier. Naja had wanted the divorce more than Max. Because Axel was so young when they split up, and because Naja had taken care of him most of the time when he was a baby, he was closest to her. Max had trouble accepting that he couldn't have Axel a week at a time, as he did Tim; he and Naja didn't at all see eye to eye on that.

Before the divorce, their marriage had been rocky. It angered Max that she didn't prioritize them as a couple, and Naja got mad at him for working too much. They clashed repeatedly over these things, and the arguments escalated until Naja decided to split up with him.

They asked the district social authorities for anonymous counseling, and they were advised to slowly increase Max's time with Axel as he grew older, in accordance with how he reacted to staying with his father. They agreed to follow this advice, and Max spent shorter but more frequent periods of time with the boy. Gradually Axel felt more comfortable being with him, and by the time he was three years old, he was accompanying his older brother on exchange days.

Visitation Rights Can Be Adjusted

Visitation rights can change over time. They should mirror the needs of the children, to help make their everyday lives smoother as well as ensuring a strong, secure bond to both parents. Such a bond doesn't require co-parents to divide the time up equally. It is important, however, that both parents are accessible to and give their attention to the children when they are with them, and that the collaborative atmosphere is good. It's also important that the children trust their parents.

It's also common that visitation rights need to be very flexible for children like Tim and Axel as they get older, to accommodate their teenage lives.

The Common Basis - Loving the Children

As described in earlier chapters, when a divorce occurs, it requires work to accept your emotional reactions and take responsibility for your actions.

For a long time, Max was angry at Naja for what he felt was unfair treatment concerning Axel. When Naja found another partner, it made things even more difficult for him. His sister spoke with him several times and allowed him to vent, which helped him focus on working with Naja. He loved his kids very much, and he chose to base his actions on that. Naja had an easier time getting through the breakup, perhaps because she was the one who wanted the divorce in the first place. Her anger toward Max faded, especially after she found someone else. They saw how their collaboration went more smoothly when they shared experiences they'd had with their kids. Focusing on this was what helped them the most.

Diversity is a Strength

Naja and Max both found out, each in their own way, that the basis of their collaboration was their shared love for their children. As a result, it became easier to reach agreements with each other. *In the time leading up to the divorce, Naja was very angry with Max. She often thought she might just as easily be a single mother, since he was working so much. She also felt the kids probably wouldn't even miss him, given how distracted and distant he was. Max was also angry with her, because he felt she was simply too much as a mother, that she smothered the boys, and that this wasn't good for either of them. He felt the best thing for the boys was to live with him most of the time. Fortunately, the counseling sessions they took changed both their outlooks. It became clear to Naja that Max was good with the boys in some ways she never could be. He might not be the best at comforting them and supporting them emotionally, but he took an active role in their lives. The boys adored him when he felt like playing games with them. And Max saw that in comparison to him, Naja was extremely caring with the boys, good at handling things Tim was having trouble with in school, for instance. Max simply didn't spot things like that. Even though she had stricter rules than he did about screen time and bedtimes, he respected her ability to structure and organize the boys' lives.*

In time they both felt more at ease with the situation. They realized how important each other was for Axel and Tim. But to get to that place, it was first necessary for them to make peace with the past.

The Past Can't Be Changed

At one point, Naja was very bitter toward Max, some of it dating back to episodes in the past. To her his somewhat lax attitude toward criti-

cism made him seem apathetic. Originally, she had fallen for his calm demeanor, his ability to not let things get under his skin, traits that drove her up the wall later when they were married. Part of what she had to go through was to accept her anger with him and at the same time let go of it. This was much easier for her to do after they broke up. Max went through a similar process. Naja criticized him a lot, said he worked too much, that he hadn't changed Axel's diaper, that he forgot to buy milk. What she didn't realize was that all this criticism made him feel bad. She simply couldn't see what Max was going through, all the anger piling up inside him that led him to distance himself from her. Just after the divorce, he couldn't at all see that they would ever be able to work together well, but after some talks with his sister, he realized there were things he couldn't change. He had to accept that she'd made him mad. He could see that being clearer about what was important to him helped Naja relax.

Their collaboration became much easier. In time, Naja and Max were both able to make peace with their past.

Everyone Profits From a Good Collaboration

Naja and Max had to seek help to create a better collaborative atmosphere. They were offered a course that focused on cooperation. They learned about children's reactions to divorce, how they could work together better, and how important it was to take care of yourself after a divorce. The course ended with a discussion that improved their collaboration, which they clearly saw helped their children too. Following the divorce, Tim had a shorter fuse than usual and was involved in more conflicts at school. He also got mad at Axel about small, insignificant things. After his parents took the course, he settled down. He also stopped staying in his room by himself so much.

At one point, Naja and Max got together and looked back on the time immediately preceding and following the divorce. They realized they had been in a very difficult place back then, and they were relieved that the hostility they'd shown each other no longer steered their collaboration.

Take Responsibility for Your Reactions

Naja and Max agreed that the support they'd received from others had been vital in getting them back on the path to a decent collaboration. Max had spoken a lot to his sister, and Naja had been given help and support by several of her girlfriends. They decided to do everything in their power to stay on that positive path.

Agreements

To make sure you continue to work together well, agreeing on some good principles is important. *After the course on cooperation, Naja and Max met with a family counselor. Together they set down some rules about their collaboration. Such things require time, and it took several meetings to work everything out.*

Speak in Positive Terms About Your Ex

The first rule they came up with was to always speak about each other in positive terms around the children. They recognized that involv-

ing their kids in any disagreements they might have would only cause problems for the kids. They also agreed to speak well of each other to their networks. Naja was aware that her father didn't get along with Max, therefore she avoided talking to him about her frustrations with her ex. When Max simply became too much for her, she vented to an old friend who could handle her being totally one-sided about him. After things had improved between them, however, all that wasn't so necessary anymore.

Treat Each Other With Respect

The next agreement they made was to treat each other with respect. This meant first discussing with each other issues having to do with the health and well-being of the children. Naja and Max would both feel bad, for example, if one of them introduced Tim and Alex to a new boyfriend or girlfriend without first talking to the other about it.

Keep Agreements

A third important rule was that they would stick to their specific agreements. Naja had been enraged at Max a few times when he returned the children a day earlier than usual without informing her about it beforehand. Once a friend of his had invited him for a night out, and he felt he couldn't say no, because they hadn't seen each other in a long time. Naja had been forced to break off a weekend with her mother, and the episode had been a sore spot between them for quite a while. From then on, therefore, all their agreements were to be kept. They did agree, however, that in cases where an acute or serious situation came up, rule number four would come into effect.

Be Flexible

It was important to Max that they could be flexible with each other. He was very frustrated when he couldn't take the boys along to his mother's sixtieth birthday, because it was on a day they were with Naja. She'd planned on taking them to an amusement park. This was not long after their divorce, and Naja said she'd been angry with Max because of the aforementioned night on the town with his friend, when he'd brought the boys to her a day early.

Their discussion about future agreements led them to the realization that focusing on what was good for the kids was the important thing. Which is why the fourth rule, being flexible when possible, was an important priority.

Share Concerns About the Children

Naja also wanted them to promise to be better at sharing their thoughts and concerns about how the kids were doing. Back when Tim was having trouble in school, Max had spoken with his class teacher. They had decided that Tim should talk to the teacher when he was feeling bad in class. Naja wasn't informed about this decision, and Tim had already talked with his teacher a few times before Naja found out about it. That led to a lot of confusion, and Naja was of course also unhappy that they had made the decision without her.

Seek Help and Support

The final point in their overall agreement was that they would seek help if their collaboration became difficult in the future. What they had learned from the counseling about cooperation had convinced them that it could be necessary to get professional help, if a problem came up that they weren't able to resolve themselves.

PITFALLS

When You Don't Seek Help in Time

It's especially challenging – yet necessary to your collaboration – to be able to trust a co-parent. If you disagreed about the breakup, and if one or both of you are emotionally affected by it, it can be difficult to have faith in each other.

A stable and satisfactory collaborative atmosphere is vital to the well-being of your children, and to ensure it you must be able to trust each other to treat the children well and want what's best for them. You also need to have mutual respect. If you can't count on your co-parent, the mood when you're working together is going to suffer for it. And if problems with the collaboration arise, they can blow up into a conflict. You might not feel like being flexible (as a form of revenge), and your frustration with your ex will take over the reins of the collaboration. Emotions will dominate, and your window of tolerance will shrink. Finally, all dialogue between you will stop, and you'll form a negative, conflict-filled dynamic that puts a strain on everyone, especially the children.

When this sort of dynamic crops up, it's important to talk about the specific problems involved and the reason for the change in behavior, in order to de-escalate the conflict. You may need help from people in your network who can be impartial, or you can also seek professional help. Remember that disagreements are okay, they are a completely natural part of being parents, divorced or not. The important thing is to prevent them from becoming gridlocked.

QUESTIONS TO ASK YOURSELF

- How is your collaboration on the children going at the moment?
- How can you make sure it stays okay in the future?
- What's important to you when you have to cooperate with your co-parent?
- What's important to your co-parent when they have to cooperate with you?

Outline for a typical collaboration discussion

We share:

- A love for our children and the wish to create the best conditions for them to do well in their childhood and teenage years, which will provide them with the best opportunities for having a good adult life.

We acknowledge:

- That our children need us to work together, to create the best conditions for them to mature and develop.
- That our children need both of us, with the strengths and weaknesses we each have.
- That we can't change the problematic collaboration and experiences we had in the past.
- That these experiences have taken their toll on both of us as well as our children.
- That we can't change each other as parents, but we can recognize the strengths in our differences.

Therefore we agree:

- That we will never speak badly of our co-parent in front of our children.
- That from now on we will treat each other and each other's network with respect.

- That we will honor the agreements we make.

- That we will be flexible whenever possible.

- That we will take responsibility for seeking help should we need it.

- That in situations where we need to change an agreement, we will set aside enough time to find a solution – and seek outside help if it proves to be too difficult for us to solve.

- That if we are worried about how our children are doing, we will talk about it and find the best possible way to support them.

- That we will seek help if talking things over and our collaboration become too difficult.

(Make your own collaboration agreement – write down more points to agree on)

CHAPTER 10

When Other Circumstances
Are At Stake

CENTRAL IDEAS IN THIS CHAPTER

- Children with special needs put greater demands on parenthood and the collaboration between parents.

- Long-lasting gridlocked conflicts can be solved.

- Agree on a realistic amount of time together between a child and a vulnerable parent, so they can form a good relationship.

This chapter deals with divorces involving special circumstances. In such cases, the recommendations central to the other chapters of this book have to be adjusted. A focus is put on three areas: divorces where there is a child with special needs involved, divorces that drag out and are full of conflict, and di-

vorces where one parent's ability to take adequate care of the children is a serious concern.

Children With Special Needs

Children have various degrees of sensitivity. Some are robust, others are easily affected. And within these degrees, there are children with special needs. Some of them have diagnoses, others don't, but regardless, they are challenged to an extent that it requires a special effort from parents to meet these needs and help them mature as well as possible (Loft, 2011).

Morten and Klara

Morten and Klara have two children, Emil and Anna, six years old and two-and-a-half years old respectively at the time of the divorce. Emil was a happy schoolboy; he played soccer, traded Pokémon cards. He was doing fine. Anna was a different story, however. Her birth had been difficult, and she had suffered hypoxia, a lack of oxygen. She was lagging behind in her verbal skills, and her day care center was worried. Klara was convinced that Anna would catch up, but Morten was concerned. Anna didn't sleep well at night, and it was hard to comfort her. With time it became obvious that Anna wasn't developing like other children, and she was given a diagnosis.

Morten and Klara were exhausted from all the tests they had gone through with Anna, and they didn't feel they'd gotten enough support and help from the district. Their relationship became so strained that finally they saw no alternative to divorce.

The biggest challenge to their collaboration after the divorce was that they were very different as parents. Klara was totally focused on being there for Anna, and she had a hard time accepting Morten's tendency to downplay Anna's special needs. He didn't think he needed the Special-Ed guidelines they were both given. Whenever Anna came back to Klara after staying with Morten, she reacted violently the first few days. He'd been very absorbed in his work, and he focused more on Emil when the two kids were with him.

The teachers in the Special Needs day care center where Anna had started were concerned about how she was doing in the weeks she was with Morten. Her development regressed, and she began biting and hitting the other children. She was obviously more frustrated. The day care center called her parents in for a conference, where they voiced their concern. Klara got angry and frustrated with Morten for not pulling himself together and heeding the advice they'd been given by the Special-Ed teacher. Morten felt he had a natural, intuitive way of interacting with Anna, and he also believed he was following the general advice he'd read about on the internet concerning Special-Ed children. The day care expressed their concerns to the district.

More Similar Styles of Parenting

It takes more to be a satisfactory parent when a child has special needs. And it's especially important for the child's parents to adopt similar styles of parenting.

Morten and Klara's story shows how being a parent of children with special needs is a bigger job. Morten's style of parenting would likely be okay for a child with normal needs, but with a child like Anna, it's vital that parents follow the guidelines set down by professionals.

It was very difficult for Morten to handle having a child with special needs. He tried not to think about it, to focus instead on his work and Emil's soccer. He hadn't dealt with the difficult emotions and the crisis that having a child with special needs always creates. The divorce was also tough on Morten, and he felt enormous pressure on the days he had both kids.

Greater Need for an Oxygen Mask

Morten and Klara both needed to do more work on their oxygen masks – that is, it was paramount for them to take better care of themselves. *During her weeks without the kids, Klara worked on dealing with her painful emotions. The divorce was hard enough, and the extra burden of being a parent to a child with special needs made it vital that she spend more time working on herself. Morten, on the other hand, buried himself in his work and tried to ignore the difficult thoughts and emotions. Finally, when the district offered to send someone to help with Anna for a day now and then, both he and Klara accepted.*

Greater Need for Collaboration

The district also offered them couples therapy to help out with their collaboration. During the sessions, they agreed on several points. Exchange days and Anna's general need for continuity when it came to meals and bedtime routines were important issues, and they agreed on practices to help in those areas. The mood between them when working together also improved. And Emil began talking more about problems he sometimes faced in school, which he'd been holding back.

When Special Circumstances Arise Later

It can be even more challenging for co-parents when their child develops special needs after a divorce. They may have to modify their collaboration, such as working together in a closer and more coordinated manner than they are used to, sometimes after finally sorting things out following a difficult divorce. It can be hard enough when a child suddenly develops special needs, from an illness, for example, and having to deal with changes in a collaboration can make it even more necessary to focus on your own oxygen mask.

Many co-parents also find themselves in a dilemma when they discuss concerns about the child's welfare with the other parent. Will their co-parent feel they're being criticized; will they fall back into a contentious collaboration? Should they keep their worries to themselves, given the consequences that sharing them might have? It might be a good idea to discuss and agree on how to deal with such thorny situations before they arise, as well as whether or not to seek professional help.

When Conflicts Drag Out

In my practice as a psychologist, I've met many divorced parents trapped in a long, drawn-out conflict. It's always painful to witness, because of all the frustration, bitterness, and helplessness felt by the parents. They are worn out, and often their perception of the other parent is rigid, set in stone. When I speak to a parent alone, I can always sense their love for their children. The two parents' stories are often very similar when they speak about the central issue in their conflict with the other parent.

Albert and Runa

Albert and Runa split up ten years ago. Their child, Maja, was two years old at the time. During those first two years, Albert and Runa sometimes lived together, sometimes not, until Runa found a new partner and moved in with him. After that, their collaboration on Maya became very difficult. Several times a year they contacted the district social authorities because of their disagreements about visitation rights, vacations, where they were living, who would sign her passport, etc. Over the years, Maya had spoken many times to social workers and in court, where she explained how she was doing with each of her parents and how she felt about the current visitation rights.

Runa felt Albert was a bitter man who only wanted to punish her. Albert, on the other hand, thought Runa was always trying to prevent him and Maya from getting along well together.

The Negative Pattern

Gradually the problems her parents had in working together began to take their toll on Maya. She never talked to either of them about what she'd been doing with the other parent, and the icy atmosphere between them affected her. Maya's dream was that her parents could be good friends, but she knew that was never going to happen. Their terrible relationship wore her down. Meanwhile Runa and Albert's long, constant battle drained them, and they became increasingly embittered with each other. They both talked to their respective networks about how the other was a bad parent, how they could see that Maya was suffering because of the other's parenting skills. They were trapped in a negative pattern that sapped their strength and stamina and was harming Maya.

Children Who Choose One Parent

Long-term unresolved conflicts often result in a child feeling so overwhelmed from being caught in the middle that they finally feel forced to take sides.

When Maja was thirteen, she couldn't take any more of being involved in her parents' conflict. She chose to live permanently with her father and break off contact with her mother.

It happens once in a while that a child in serious need of peace, harmony, and a normal life resorts to this drastic step. Such an extreme, radical act stems from the child or teenager feeling they have to cut one parent out of their life for the sake of their own emotional health. It's a survival strategy.

The Need for Both Parents

It's the same type of assessment commonly made by professionals. Judges and social authorities sometimes ask professionals to evaluate a child in cases where there is doubt about what visitation rights or physical custody rights are best for the child. A decision is made about how adversely a child is being affected by the parents' inability to cooperate, after which it is weighed against the child's need for a connection to both parents. If the conflict has lasted a long time and is overwhelming the child, it can end with a significant reduction or even suspension of visitation rights for one parent. This happens only in the worst of circumstances, of course, but it's worth mentioning, because it gives a picture of how a long-term conflict between parents has no winners. Luckily, there are methods for bringing these conflicts to an end.

Focus on the Needs of the Children

A Dutch psychologist, Justine van Lawick (2015), has developed an extremely effective method to help divorced parents out of an ugly, long-lasting conflict. The method involves several parents being assisted simultaneously; in a sense, they help each other. One of the best ways to bring about change is through a series of exercises in which parents experience how it feels to be a child caught in a conflict between parents. It's almost a physical feeling, being in the child's shoes, and it pushes parents to change how they treat their co-parent. The goal isn't for them to become good friends and acknowledge each other; less can do the trick. They just need to not speak badly about each other, in order to help the children.

The most important point in this section is that it's never too late to change a bad pattern of interaction. Improving a collaboration – or not – affects children greatly. When parents are able to cooperate better, it shows their children something important: that even though it can be hard, their parents' relationship can improve. It shows them that change is a possibility, that conflicts don't have to last forever.

Serious Concern With the Other Parent

This section briefly outlines the greatest worries involved when there's a serious concern about one of the parents in a divorce. Several of this situation's central aspects – not all, of course, but several – are examined.

Parents trapped in a conflict that drags out for several years are often worn down by long-term stress. Gradually they become worse versions of themselves, from being strongly affected by overactive fight-or-flight hormones. Even if you take care of yourself, a conflict can be so overwhelming that your emotional window of tolerance becomes very small. Unfortunately, this damages your ability to do your job as a parent.

Other parents may have personalities that in general are vulnerable. Their window of tolerance is low to begin with; therefore it takes very little for them to be overly emotionally affected. They then have trouble thinking clearly and keeping their emotions in check.

Lasse and Camilla

Lasse and Camilla have been divorced for several years. Their daughter, Mathilde, is nine years old and in sixth grade. She loves her youth club, where many of her friends from school go. Lasse and Camilla have always had problems with their collaboration. Lasse has primary physical custody of Mathilde. Camilla has her two days every two weeks, and she's very dissatisfied with this situation. She feels she should have Mathilde half of the time. The district authorities and the court, however, don't agree. Their assessment of what was best for Mathilde led to the present agreement. Camilla has had some very unstable periods in her life due to alcohol abuse, when she was very emotionally erratic.

The Strength and Energy Needed To Be a Parent

If a parent has a personal weakness or problem that affects their capacity and ability to do okay as a parent, agreements about visitation rights must take that into account. It's important that the time a parent and child spend together supports the well-being and development of the child. It's better to have shorter and more frequent periods together that are generally positive, as opposed to fewer long periods.

A Swedish social worker, Kari Killén (2005), outlined a number of parental capabilities, one of which is relevant here: that you as a parent can control your emotions, that any anger you feel toward others, for example your ex, isn't taken out on your children, either directly or by denigrating your co-parent. It's normal that occasionally you lose your temper and speak sharply to your children, even though you're angry at someone else. When it happens, it's important to make up to your children and take on parental responsibility, so your anger doesn't cause real harm to them.

Camilla had trouble gathering the strength and energy to be there for Mathilde. When she wasn't feeling well, once in a while she took her anger out on her daughter over silly things. Later on, she was well aware of what she had done, and she felt guilty about yelling so much at her. Mathilde didn't tell anyone about her mother's outbursts, until one day she broke down when talking to her class teacher; she admitted that whenever she went to stay with her mother, she got a stomach ache.

The Ability to Comply With Visitation Rights

Another central issue for troubled parents is whether they're able to comply with visitation rights. If an agreed-upon time with a child is canceled or postponed several times, the child becomes insecure and disappointed and wonders if the parent cares about and loves them. If it happens too often, it's a sign that the visitation rights need to be adjusted, so that the parent can hold up their end of the agreement and the child can then count on the parent.

Eventually the periods when Mathilde lived with Camilla stabilized. There had been a time when Camilla canceled often, and it became too much for Lasse. He needed to be able to plan his free weekends, and he could see that Mathilde was affected by her mother's cancellations. Sometimes she felt her mother didn't care about her.

Abuse

District authorities take it very seriously when one parent has a substance abuse problem. A parent being under the influence of drugs or alcohol during a visitation constitutes legal grounds for blocking the parent's visitation rights. For visitations to resume, often the parent has to go through treatment.

During one of the periods when Camilla regularly canceled the times she was to have Mathilde, she often hit the bars in town and went full Monty, as she put it. A binge could last several days. When she finally pulled out of her tailspin, she didn't have the energy to be with Mathilde during the considerable time it took her to recover. As a result of her instability, Lasse and Camilla had a meeting with the social authorities. Lasse expressed his concern about all her cancellations, and the district decided that in order to keep her visitation rights, Camilla would have to go through treatment for her substance abuse problem. At first Camilla refused, and all contact between her and Mathilde was suspended.

Children's Need to Know Their Parents

Even when a parent has a personality-related problem or an emotional illness that affects their ability to be a full-time parent, in the vast majority of cases it's important for children to get to know this parent. Children who don't know one of their parents seldom develop a nuanced picture of them, and they may end up either demonizing or idealizing them. A multi-faceted picture of our parents, including their strengths and weaknesses, gives us the sense that we know them. And it creates the foundation for knowing and understanding ourselves and our personalities.

If a child loses contact with one parent, as in Mathilde's case, it's important that their co-parent maintain a nuanced picture of them. It's also important to tell the child that it's not his or her fault, which many children believe, and that it's natural to feel anger, helplessness, and a longing for that parent.

It was hard on Mathilde to have so many mixed feelings about her mother, and for a long time she told no one about all the many troubling things that happened while she stayed with her mother, because she didn't want to be disloyal to her. Fortunately, after a few months Camilla decided to go into rehab, after which visitations with her daughter were permitted again.

Camilla became a better and more stable parent to Mathilde.

Where Can You Get Special Help and Support?

Some divorces are complicated, and they require parents to act quickly and get the right help and support. Some parents need more intensive support. Again, the most important thing is that parents get help quickly with difficult divorces, so conflicts don't become deadlocked and even more difficult to resolve. Private and public organizations that provide help and support exist in most countries.

QUESTIONS TO ASK YOURSELF

- How do you take care of yourself when being a parent of a child with special needs gets to be too much for you?

- How will you ensure that your child can hope your long deadlocked conflict with your co-parent will improve?

- How do you ensure that your vulnerable co-parent plays as clear a role in your child's life as possible?

- Are you sure that your co-parent lacks parenting abilities, that you're not demonizing them unfairly?

AFTERWORD

There's Hope for Everyone

My wish is that this book has given you a sense of hope. Even though your situation may look dismal, ways exist in which you can create a satisfactory collaboration with your co-parent.

If you take care of yourself, to have the strength and energy to do your job as a parent and cooperate with your co-parent; if you seek emotional and practical support when needed, to free up the energy needed to make it through the hard times; and if you form a realistic level of cooperation with your co-parent and agree on ways to help maintain it, you will have created a strong, resilient foundation for both of you to get through the divorce without anyone falling to pieces.

Even if you are deadlocked in a long, complicated divorce, and all hope seems lost, it's still possible to find help and eventually get to a better place in your life.

ACKNOWLEDGMENTS

This book could not have been written without the contributions of several people who have influenced it in various ways. Thanks to Signe Lindskov Hansen, editor-in-chief, and Signe Gottlieb, editor, for their valuable input on the book's form, target group, content, and style. I would also like to thank the Center for Family Development, in particular the fine people I worked with in their divorce division.

I owe a great deal of gratitude to Søren Marcussen and Rikke Cecilie Toft Dejour for the rewarding experiences we had in the "Parents Together – Separately" project, and the reflections we shared about it.

Thanks also to Rikke Hermansen, Else Marie Schmidt Andersen, and Dragana Mateskovic for our fruitful collaboration on the "Shared Children – Whole Children" project.

The book also could not have been written without the professional superstars in couples and divorce therapy I have met: psychologist and couples therapist Jette Simon, psychologist Justine van Lawick, and psychologist and researcher Frode Thuen. I'd also like to include the founder of the Center for Family Development, Annette Due Madsen, for her enthusiasm and dedication to making the well-being and development of children a priority.

I'm grateful to Kristoffer Munk and Lars Paludan-Müller for contributing with professional perspectives on the book.

Finally, this book would never have been written if not for the willingness of several divorced parents I know to contribute with their personal experiences and perspectives: Anne Hougaard Thygesen, Jesper Fredslund-Andersen, Kristina Hedemann, Peter Aagaard, Lise Blandt, Ida Hansen, and Nina Qvistgaard.

And thanks to my family, Katrine, Noah, and Astrid, who have tolerated my periods of inattentiveness and distraction when my work and projects took up too much of my life.

BIBLIOGRAPHY

Amato, P.R. (2012). The consequences of divorce for adults and children: An update. Journal of General Social Issues, 23, 1.

Bilenberg, N., Christiansen, E., Petersen, D.J., Nielsen, L.G., and Rasmussen, C.S. (2014). Adverse life events as risk factors for behavioral and emotional problems in a seven-year follow-up of a population-based child cohort. Nordic Journal of Psychiatry, 64: 1-7.

Børns Vilkår (2016). Børn i komplekse skilsmisser - en kvalitativ undersøgelse af børns oplevelser af komplekse skilsmisser (Children in complex divorces – a qualitative investigation of how children experience complex divorces). Downloaded at bornsvilkar.dk

Circle of Security's manual. https://vidensportal.dk/temaer/Omsorgssvigt/indsatser/Circle-of-security-2013-parenting-cos-p

Gran, S. (2016). It's over – the story of separation. Copenhagen: Aschehoug Publishing.

Hartley, S.L., Barker, E.T., Seltzer, M.M., Floyd, F., Greenberg, J., Orsmond, G., and Bolt, D. (2010). The relative risk and timing of divorce in families of children with an autism spectrum disorder. Journal of Family Psychology, 24(4):449-457.

Hermansen, R., Marcussen, S., Schmidt Andersen, E.M., Sindberg, T.H., Thuen, F., and Ringkøbing Rothenberg, J. (eds.) (2014). Children's group manual, "Shared Children – Whole Children," borne-gruppen.dk, Center for Family Development, Egmont Fund.

Johnson, S. (2015). Hold me – a road map for lasting love. Copenhagen: Mindspace Publishing.

Killén, K. (2005). Parental neglect is everyone's responsibility. Copenhagen: Hans Reitzels Publishing.

Kristensen, J.K. (2014). Dad is angry, because he's afraid of being abandoned: Concerning divorces with serious conflicts, seen in an attachment theory frame of understanding. Matrix, 31, 3.

Lawick, J. van and Visser, M. (2015). No kids in the middle: Dialogical and creative work with parents and children in the context of high conflict divorces. Journal of Family Therapy, 36, 33-50.

Loft, L.T. (2011). Child health and parental relationships: Examining relationship termination among Danish parents with and without a child with disabilities or chronic illness. International Journal of Sociology, 4, 1.

Madsen, A.D. (ed.) (2012). Dad, Mom, and divorce – on being the children caught in the middle. Copenhagen: Danish Psychology Publishing.

Moxness, K. (2004). Gentle divorces – with the focus on the child. Copenhagen: Hans Reitzels Publishing.

Nordanger, D.Ø. and Braarud, H.C. (2014). Regulation as a key concept and window of tolerance as a model in contemporary trauma psychology. Journal of the Norwegian Psychology Association, 51, 531-536.

Ottesen, M.H. and Stage, S. (2010). Children's welfare and well-being. Copenhagen: The National Center for Social Research, SFI.

Sander, S. (2012). The ugly divorce – an empirical study of 971 divorced Danes. Psychology Institute, Copenhagen University.

Schut, M. and Stroebe, M. (2010). The dual process model of coping with bereavement: A decade on. Omega, 61, 4.

The Danish Health Agency, brochure: Men also have emotional problems.
www.sst.dk/~/media/A4BBC3A43872481F8521D964C3F877A7.ashx

Toft Dejour, R., Marcussen, S., Kristensen, J.K., and Luduch Mateskovic, D. (2017). Seminar in Shared Parental Responsibility Handbook, "The meeting with the divorced family." Copenhagen: Center for Family Development.

Vindeløv, V. (2013). Conflict resolution – a reflexive model. Copenhagen: Danish Association of Lawyers and Economists Publishing.

Øvreeide, H. (2009). Speaking with children – methodological conversations with children in difficult life situations. Copenhagen: Hans Reitzels Publishing.

ABOUT THE AUTHOR

Jan Kaa Kristensen is a certified psychologist and specialist in clinical psychology. For over ten years he has worked with divorced parents and their children, in his private practice as well as in the public sphere as an expert in child psychology. He is the former leader of the divorce division of the Center for Family Development and of two projects, "Parents Together – Separately" and "Shared Children – Whole Children." He also teaches professionals who work with divorced families. He was appointed by the Minister of Social Affairs to be a member of the advisory committee for The Family Court House in Denmark.

See more at jankaa.dk.

Printed in Poland
by Amazon Fulfillment
Poland Sp. z o.o., Wrocław

71289674R00092